Looking for Trouble

THE ADVENTURES OF
THE GEORGE BOYS

Ronnie Ridley George

EAKIN PRESS ❦ Fort Worth, Texas
www.EakinPress.com

Cover photo: *Larry, Ronnie, and Mike George on a Civil War cannon at Vicksburg, Mississippi, in the early 1950s. Photo by Dorris George.*

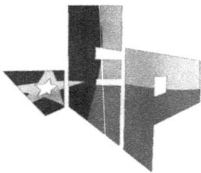

Copyright © 2008
By Ronnie Ridley George
Published By Eakin Press
An Imprint of Wild Horse Media Group
P.O. Box 331779
Fort Worth, Texas 76163
1-817-344-7036
www.EakinPress.com
ALL RIGHTS RESERVED
1 2 3 4 5 6 7 8 9
ISBN-10: 1-09-413044-3
ISBN-13: 978-1-940130-44-6

Cover pictures: Sneakers by Georgii Dolgykh, picture frame by Maksym Yemelyanov of Dreamstime.com

This book
is dedicated to:

The memory of my parents,
Cecil and Dorris George,
who worked hard all of their lives
and raised three adventurous sons
who all became
U. S. Air Force officers.

Larry, Mike, and Ronnie George, three brothers who all became U.S. Air Force officers, with "Old Blue," the family's 1950 Chevy.

—Photo by Dorris George

Contents

Foreword

Trouble. What is trouble? More often than not, it is the one thing we hate to see or the one event most dreaded. What we don't see is that trouble provides excitement in our lives. It brings about change. Sometimes that change is external but more often, it is the internal changes that we take with us through life. Those internal changes mold us, shape us, and transform us into who we are today. Whether good or bad, trouble is what determines the kind of people we are and who we are to become. It brings out the best and the worst in us at the most inopportune moments. Without trouble, we would have no stories; no tales to tell our children. Without trouble, we would have no desire to advance spiritually, emotionally, or physically. It is what defines our very essence. It is what urges us forward.

In life, we only have a small amount of time to get things right and make good use of what we are blessed to have. The friendships we make and choices we choose are what creates our very being, our soul if you will. If not for the trouble we got into growing up, I do not know how we would have turned out, for it was those times when problems arose that demanded we show our true colors; rise to the occasion or fail in misery. I do not mean to say that every day is a life-or-death choice or that every moment will determine our destiny. I simply am saying that each little decision to each little trial in life is what knocks off the rough edges and makes us streamlined and built for high speed—the speed of life.

Ronnie George and I have been friends since junior high school, and we have been looking for trouble together ever since. I cherish the memories of those joyous times at the George Farm and Ronnie's great parents. *Looking for Trouble* is a wonderful tribute to Ron's loving parents, his amazing brothers, a great farm, and a time when we all were brilliant, good looking, and sexy as heck. Not all of our friends knew that of course.

Looking for Trouble is a compilation of stories providing a great walk down memory lane and bringing back thoughts of a simpler time when trouble lurked in the most unsuspecting places. As I read this book, I could not help thinking back to those days of wonder and smiling about the fun we had as mischief-ridden teenage youths of Greenville, Texas—riding bicycles, playing backyard basketball, hunting at the George Farm, and cruising Lee Street. We had that Rockwell-ian youth that now exists only in tales of yore. It is a read that harkens back to a time when the loss of innocence did not come at such a young age and the horrors of life were kept at bay just a wee bit longer. *Looking for Trouble* is a good read for the person who longs for the days when getting out of trouble was just as much fun as getting into trouble.

—Fred E. Bennett, Jr.
Captain, USAF (Ret.)

Preface

I come from a long line of story-tellers, but then most people did in the days before radio and television. As a boy, I would sit quietly on the front porch or under a shade tree in the cool of a summer evening or by the warm fireplace on a cold winter day and listen to my family and the neighbors telling and retelling tales of long ago. The old folks did most of the talking. The youngsters were supposed to listen quietly or go play somewhere else.

My mother, Dorris Ridley George, from Campbell, near Greenville in Northeast Texas, and her family kept a remarkable verbal and written history of living family members and of our ancestors. My Uncle Bob, the late Reverend Robert H. Ridley, a Methodist minister for more than seventy years, was one of the family's historians. Uncle Bob often spoke of our ancestor Bishop Nicholas Ridley who was burned at the stake in Oxford, England, in 1555 as though the ashes were still warm.

Mom told stories of our cousin Nathan Hale's capture and execution as a spy by the British during the American Revolution and of her grandfather, Confederate Captain Robert Ridley's wounding and capture by the Yankees near Vicksburg during the Civil War. She said Captain Ridley was later imprisoned near Chicago where some of the prisoners ate rats to survive. Captain Ridley said he just wasn't that hungry himself. Captain Ridley survived the Civil War but died during the influenza epidemic of 1918. Mom told these stories as though these events had just happened.

Mom also repeated stories about her great-grandparents coming to Texas in 1837 and 1849 and of the Indians, bears, and bushwhackers they found there. She also told of her own childhood memories of farm life, runaway horses, traveling circuses, wandering bands of Gypsies, of gathering pecans, picking cotton, smoking hams, making sausages, and cooking boiled custard.

My daddy, Cecil George, told stories about his boyhood at Van, Texas, near Tyler. Daddy told me that when he was a small boy, he was walking along an unpaved street in Van with his school teacher. Recalling a story they had read in class, Daddy said, "Teacher, do you think there is gold under the ground where we are walking?" His teacher said, "No, Cecil, I don't think so." Later after Grandpaw George moved the family to Campbell, black gold was discovered on the farm he had sold back in Van.

Another of my favorite stories was about Daddy's Uncle Horace Thompson. Uncle Horace was a farmer who lived near Van at the time oil was first discovered there around 1930. Most of the farmers were talking about leasing their oil rights and getting rich. Uncle Horace wanted no part of that. He had a farm to run. He also had a pair of domestic geese that kept wandering off. Someone down at the post office said they had seen his geese over at a neighbor's, and Uncle Horace set out on foot to get them and bring them home. He caught the geese without too much trouble, and he was walking home down the sandy road with a big goose under each arm. He was holding each goose by the neck out in front so the goose couldn't get away or bite a plug out of him when he saw a car coming down the road toward him.

Cars were not common then at Van, and as the car got closer, Uncle Horace recognized the driver of the Model T Ford as an oilman who had been pestering him to lease his oil rights. Sure enough, the oilman pulled up to Uncle Horace, shut off his noisy engine, and started talking to Uncle Horace through the open window. Uncle Horace didn't have time for this. He had a goose under each arm, it was getting late, and he had cows to milk back home. The oilman wouldn't quit talking, and Uncle Horace kept trying to get away, but common courtesy wouldn't allow him to just walk off and leave someone who was talking to him.

The oilman eventually got around to making another offer for the drilling rights. Uncle Horace refused the offer and turned to walk away thinking the conversation was over when the oil man stopped him and said, "Just what would you take?" In desperation, Uncle Horace named a figure that has since been lost to family history but would be like us today saying "a million dollars!" The oilman immediately said, "Sold!" When Uncle Horace regained his composure, he looked down and realized he had choked both of his geese to death.

As a boy, I was concerned that I would never have stories to match those my folks were telling. After reading my ramblings, you may agree. Time and place, however, changes many things, and even ordinary stories from the Twentieth Century may be of interest to those in the Twenty-first.

Looking for Trouble is about the adventures my brothers and I had while growing up in Northeast Texas and the exciting times we had then and later in life. As youngsters, we rode on steam engines, swiped watermelons, robbed bees, rode horses, herded cattle, drove tractors, swam with snakes, and shocked our friends. All three of us served as U.S. Air Force officers. Larry specialized in laboratory medicine and computers in the Biomedical Sciences Corps. He and his family later survived Hurricane Katrina. Mike was an Air Force "Hurricane Hunter" and supersonic T-38 instructor pilot who was later flying as an airline captain on the morning of 9/11. I was an Air Force KC-135 jet tanker pilot who flew combat missions in Southeast Asia and was later a wildlife biologist who roped rattlesnakes and radio-collared mountain lions. We have been looking for trouble and adventure all our lives.

Acknowledgments

I gratefully acknowledge the assistance of all those who waded through early drafts of this book and provided valuable comments. I am especially grateful to my mother Dorris Ridley George (now deceased), my brothers Larry and Mike George, Larry's wife Janice; my cousins Bob Ridley and Bill Fleming, my Iowa friends Gay and Lloyd Crim, and Texas Parks and Wildlife Department co-workers Bob Cook, Mike Berger, Jerry Cooke, Bill Harvey, Rollin MacRae, and Lydia Saldana who offered valuable insights. John Foshee assisted with song titles and lyrics. Lisa Engeling (now deceased), Nancy Gallacher, and Marla Bays helped with early editing on their lunch hour. My wife Barbara, my sons Robert and Jim, and Jim's wife Amy reviewed and provided suggestions for earlier versions of the book. My uncle Joe Hawkins, a retired Cotton Belt Railroad engineer, shared his thoughts about the railroad stories. Uncle Joe and Local History Librarian Cheryl Westhafer located old railroad photographs at the Commerce Public Library. My Greenville High School classmates Fred Bennett, Jerry Mainord, Anita Hoover Pugh, and Larry Pugh assisted with the Greenville stories. Pat Molenaar handled final review and layout of the book, and Jennifer Molenaar designed the cover.

Looking for Trouble

"A bunch of boys is like a bunch of dogs.
They can always find some trouble to get into."
—My daddy, Cecil George, c. 1955

When I was about five years old and my brother Larry was six, we sneaked off and went skinny dipping in the Little Pool at my folk's farm east of Greenville. Neither of us could swim a lick, but that didn't seem to matter since we were only planning on wading around in the waist-deep muddy water. We were splashing around with the soft mud squishing between our toes when all of a sudden I stepped off in deep hole way over my head! Somehow, I held my breath, but I couldn't think what to do. I thought I was fix'n to drown! After drifting slowly downward in the darkness, seemly forever, my feet touched the bottom of the pond. This gave me an idea, and I kicked against the bottom. I rose up toward the sunlight, but my head didn't reach the surface. After drifting all the way to the bottom a second time, I kicked hard again, but this time I kicked toward the bank. After about the third bounce off the bottom, my head finally broke the surface in shallow water, and I was able to gasp for breath. After I crawled out on the bank, Larry was mad at me. He said he had stepped in over his head, had nearly drowned, and I had not even tried to rescue him! They say the Good Lord looks out for fools, drunks, and little kids, and I guess we qualified. Larry and I never did tell my daddy about this little bit of trouble, but he might have suspected something. We were covered in mud.

My mother had never learned to swim as a child and was absolutely terrified of water so she was always saying, "Don't you boys go near the water!" Some time later, Daddy decided that Larry and I needed to learn to swim so he took us over to the pond in Doc Bedwell's woods. Daddy brought along a couple of gallon glass jugs (the kind moonshiners used) with the small top and the glass ring for a finger hold. When those jugs were tightly capped, they held enough air to make an awkward, but useable, swimming float. Sure enough, with a little practice while holding on to our glass jugs, we were kicking and splashing around in a

Larry and Ronnie at a swimming hole, 1951.
—Photo by Cecil George;
Mom wouldn't be this close to the water.

satisfactory manner and well on our way to dog paddling and real swimming.

The only problem with these swimming lessons was that Mom was still so terrified of water that she wouldn't speak to Daddy for a day or so after each swimming lesson. She must have thought this was just one more way for the George Boys to get into trouble.

Commerce Memories

"In the other gardens
And all up the vale,
From the autumn bonfires
See the smoke trail!"
—"Autumn Fires"
by Robert Louis Stevenson

My first memories as a child are of my parents, my brother Larry, and our home in Commerce, Texas. Mom was a housewife (and former school teacher, girls' basketball coach, and school principal). Daddy was a railroader. Our home was in a rented duplex (two apartments under one roof) on the west side of Maloney Street. We lived in the north side of the duplex. There was a constant turnover of renters in the other side of our duplex. The turnover might have been due to those noisy George Boys. The walls were kinda thin.

There were a lot of big sycamore trees along both sides of Maloney Street planted between the street and the sidewalk. In the fall of the year, everyone in Commerce raked up their leaves in piles and burned them in the street against the concrete curb. The whole town was smoky. When I close my eyes yet, I can still see the dense white

4

smoke and smell the damp, musty odor of burning sycamore leaves.

The trees had been there for quite a while, and their
roots had buckled the concrete sidewalks in many places,
raising some sections two or three inches higher than the
rest of the sidewalk and making for difficult tricycle riding.
Larry and I were amazed when our next door neighbors had
a new concrete sidewalk poured, and Larry said, "They
made it without cracks." We understood a little better when
we saw the workmen marking off sections in the smooth,
wet cement with a special tool.

Like everybody else who lived in Commerce in the
1940s and early '50s, we burned our household trash out
behind the house. Our burn barrel was a homemade, rec-
tangular, dark-blue, sheet-metal contraption built so a
grownup could dump trash in the top and light the fire at a
small access door at the bottom. I had a yellow plastic toy
duck, the kind that floats in the bathtub, that I carried
everywhere. One day, I was out in the yard with my plastic
duck, and it was really cold. There was a fire going in the
burn barrel. I thought I ought to warm up my duck. So I
placed him just inside the little access door at the bottom
of the barrel. In a few seconds I was horrified to see my
duck bubbling. I screamed bloody murder, and Mom came
running out and raked what was left of my duck out of the
barrel. My folks got me another plastic duck, a slightly-
larger pink one, but it was never the same.

Daddy had a huge swing set built for us at Junior
Kimball's blacksmith shop in Campbell. I remember going
down to the farm with Daddy to get some long pieces of
two-inch steel pipe to make the frame. The swing set had
two swings and two trapeze bars. Right after it was first
built, Mom sure got a black eye trying to protect one of us
from a violently swinging trapeze bar. The swing set was
painted silver, and the seats were painted blue-green. The

swing set was heavy and built to last. Generations of children have played on that swing set which still stands today at the farm where it was later moved.

I recall a lot of rain in Commerce during the winter and spring, and Mom would read to Larry and me on rainy days. I especially liked the poems and stories about animals. "The Boy Who Cried Wolf," "The Three Little Pigs," and "Higgledy Piggledy my Black Hen" were some of my favorites. We didn't have any pets then, but I remember feeding breadcrumbs to the birds. There was a red-headed woodpecker that drummed on a telephone pole over in the neighbor's yard. I could sure relate to the poem we read later in school that said, "The woodpecker pecked out a little round hole and made him a house in the telephone pole."

There was a short peach tree, a tall apple tree, and a tall wild plum tree on the fence line between us and our neighbors to the north. I only remember ripe peaches one time on the peach tree. As I recall, the apples never got red; the best they ever did was a pale green with thin red stripes. However, Larry and I sure enjoyed chunking the green apples and dipping them in a can of blue-green paint left over from the swing set project.

The plum tree was a different story; not only did it have fragrant white blossoms in the spring, but it showered down ripe (and occasionally wormy) plums when the wind blew. I believe my very first assigned chore was to pick up the good plums for Mom to make into preserves. She let me use a fancy little cut-glass bucket with a copper bail (probably one of her wedding gifts) to collect the plums. Young as I was, I recognized that was an unusual plum bucket.

We had a sandbox that Larry and I played in and the neighbor's cats used as a litter box. A person can learn a lot playing in a sandbox, but Mom was very distressed because I kept eating sand. Our doctor told her I would probably grow out of it. I guess I eventually did.

Childhood is confusing. You are constantly told, "You're too young to be doing that," "Stay out of the street," or "Don't be climbing so high in that tree!" and in the next breath they tell you, "Why don't you grow up," "Be responsible," "Act your age!" But there were also some great times too.

When I was about four years old, Mom would give me some money and send me across the street and down to the little grocery store and café on the corner of Maloney and Live Oak streets to get a quart bottle of milk. On about the second trip, the glass bottle slipped out of my hands and broke on the concrete sidewalk. I was heartbroken; I had failed to be responsible, but Mom said it was all right and not to cry.

The folks who ran the grocery store had a little rat terrier that had the bluff on me. It would wait until I got nearly to the store, and then it would come charging out yapping and nipping at my heals. I was terrified of it! There was also a huge English pointer with a missing front leg that sometimes hobbled through our yard. It took me several years to get over being afraid of dogs.

During a trip to the dentist's office when I was about five years old, I heard our dentist say, "Doggone it." Well, that was a new expression for me so I worked those words into a conversation later that day. Mom was appalled! My folks marched me into the bathroom, and Daddy washed my mouth out with Ivory soap. My, how times have changed!

When I was about six and Larry seven, Mom drove us to town and parked behind the stores on Bonham Street. She left us in the car while she did a few minutes of shopping. Her last instructions were, "Do not get out of the car." After a few minutes, Larry was out exploring. He found some nandina bushes at a nearby house that were loaded with red berries. Pretty soon, Larry was chunking nandina berries at me through the open window of the car. I responded by jumping out of the car to get my own ammunition. In just a few minutes, we had all of the red berries stripped from the bushes. Unfortunately, a neighbor lady spotted us in action and reported us to Mom when she returned to the car. We were in trouble again! I still don't like nandina bushes to this day.

I was six when my brother Mike was born. I thought he was a pain to have around. He cried a lot like all babies, but the worst part was I was no longer the baby of the family, and I was expected to help out more around the house. One day when Mike was about a year old and I was nearly seven, Mom left me alone with Mike while she went to the store. Her last instructions to me were, "Do not leave the yard!"

Well, I got bored and put Mike on the tricycle and started pushing him around the block. We were around on the backside of the block when Mike stuck his bare foot in the spokes of the front wheel of the tricycle and began to scream bloody murder. People came running from everywhere including a young couple we knew. They got Mike's foot out of the wheel and told me to take the tricycle back to the house. They said they would bring Mike. When I got back to the house without Mike, our nosey neighbor ladies said, "Where's the baby?" By the time I explained what had happened, the young couple showed up with Mike. I got Mike back in the house and thought everything was going to be OK, but as Mom was coming in the front door, the neighbors told on me. I was in trouble again!

When I was a boy, very few people had an electric refrigerator; what we had was an icebox. An icebox was an insulated, upright, wood and metal thing with three compartments. The right two compartments held milk, eggs, meat, and other perishables, and the left compartment held a block of ice to keep the food cold. The icebox had a tube

Ronnie and Larry on their tricycle, late 1940s. Don't they look sweet?
—Photo by Dorris George

which ran down through a hole in the kitchen floor to drain off the water as the ice melted. When the ice melted, the iceman delivered some more ice.

The ice company in Commerce issued a cardboard card to each household to assist the iceman with his deliveries. The card was about ten inches square and was divided into four triangles by lines drawn from each corner. Each triangle was a different color and had a number on it representing pounds of ice. Yellow might have meant a hundred pounds, dark blue seventy-five, white fifty, and red twenty-five or some other number. I learned some of my colors from that card. If Mom needed twenty-five pounds of ice, she hung the card on the front screen door so the red part of the card was on top, and the iceman could see from the street he needed to deliver twenty-five pounds of ice without having to go ask.

The iceman drove a pickup truck loaded with big blocks of ice. It had a heavy canvas cover to keep out dust and keep the ice from melting so fast. When the iceman pulled up in front of your house, he would glance at the card on the front door to see how much ice you needed. He would then use his ice pick (a sharp spike in a wooden handle like a screwdriver) to rapidly chip several deep holes in a line across the ice. The block would split along the chipped line, and the iceman would pick up the block with ice tongs (big metal hooks hinged in the middle like giant scissors) and carry the ice to the back door.

In really hot weather, he would carry the ice in a heavy leather and canvas bag with handles to keep the ice from dripping so bad. The iceman would usually holler "Iceman!" through the back screen door and then step into the kitchen and put the ice in the icebox. In the meantime, all of the children in the neighborhood had descended on the ice truck and were grabbing ice chips to suck on. The iceman usually took this in stride and even passed out ice chips to kids too small to reach into the back of the truck. Mom chipped ice from the big block in the icebox for making sweet iced tea we drank at every meal but breakfast. I recall when we finally got an electric refrigerator; Daddy said, "Well, I guess we won't need the ice card any more."

In the summer, the locusts (actually cicadas) would sing all day in the sycamore trees, the June bugs would buzz on the screened windows at night, and the screen doors would squeak and bang whenever any of the boys ran outside. The children would play and holler, and the big window fan in Daddy's window would hum while he was trying to sleep during the day so he could work at night on the railroad.

To me, however, the most exciting sound of summer was the mosquito spray truck making its rounds through the neighborhood in early evening. The pickup truck was rigged up with an incredibly noisy pump-contraption which sprayed a mixture of diesel fuel and DDT in a huge white cloud all over the neighborhood. When children heard the sprayer, they would run outside and chase the sprayer down the street through the cloud. I remember chasing the sprayer once until I couldn't see. When I stepped over to the left to get out of the cloud, I realized I was in oncoming traffic. Fortunately, the driver had slowed down as he met the spray truck, and I was able to step back into the "safety" of the spray. Other than writing silly stories in bad English, I do not seem to have suffered any permanent damage from that weekly dose of pesticide.

Grade School Days

"One bright morning in the middle of the night
two dead boys came out to fight.
Back to back they faced each other,
drew their swords and shot each other.
A deaf policeman heard the noise
and came to the rescue of the two dead boys.
If you don't believe my story's true,
ask the blind man. He saw it too."

—Third grade playground doggerel,
Commerce, Texas, c. 1952

I started school in the first grade in the Christian Church Annex building next to the Commerce High School while our new school building was being built. Larry and I walked to school every day from our house on Maloney Street. Some older boys picked on us nearly every trip. They weren't bad kids; I don't think they ever laid a hand on us, but we thought they were real bullies.

We had a "rhythm band" when I was in the first grade. Douglas Cooper, one of the bigger second grade boys, got to play the base drum. A couple of girls got to shake tambourines, one girl beat a triangle, and everyone else played "rhythm sticks." Rhythm sticks were two wooden sticks about a half inch in diameter, about a foot long, and painted green. We were instructed to beat our rhythm sticks together to the beat: "1, 2—1, 2, 3." So for two days, we beat this same rhythm over and over again; I thought this was really boring. On the third morning, I intentionally changed the beat to: "1, 2—1, 2, 3, 4." My teacher, who lived to be 103, and seemed that age at the time, didn't like my new rhythm. She moved me over and made me sit next to one of the girls who was "doing it right." I was in trouble again. It was decades before I again attempted to play a musical instrument.

About halfway through my first school year, the new W. J. Wheeler Elementary School on west Liveoak Street was completed, and Larry and I started going there. I did reasonably well in the first and second grades, but in the third grade, I really had trouble with spelling, and I decided I just wouldn't bother learning long division. My teacher was mad at me, and my folks were concerned, and I eventually passed, but I didn't like school. All of that changed in the fourth grade when I got into Mrs. Peak's class. Mrs. Peak found some good in every student. She selected me to be a lieutenant in the safety patrol, and she let me and several others bring bird pictures we had drawn to show the class every morning. I still had trouble with math, but Mrs. Peak's class was a turning point for me. I only regret I never thanked her.

All of the boys in school played softball at every recess. I was terrible at it. I simply didn't have the hand-eye coordination to catch or hit the ball. The only times I didn't strike out were when I'd hit soft grounders straight to the pitcher. I kept after it though. There weren't any other socially acceptable activities available for boys at recess. At the time, it didn't seem like I would ever be able to hit a baseball. I could not imagine that just over a dozen years later I would be flying supersonic jets.

Barbershop Education and Tadpole Love

"If you will bring me a four-legged tadpole,
I will love you forever."
—Martha Allard, fourth grader

As I was to learn, a lot of things contribute to a person's education besides the classroom. We moved to two other rent houses in Commerce, big places with nice yards on Ash Street near Wheeler School and later Locust Street near A. L. Day School, which was closer to the railroad yard. I learned a lot in those years in Commerce about barbershops, cars, gardens, rabbits, bugs, magazine subscriptions, and girls.

I found that a school boy could always continue his education at the barbershop. Men talk differently when there are no women around. I learned several new words while waiting for a haircut, but, remembering the Ivory soap treatment, I was careful where I used them. Barbershops also had lots of reading material that didn't include the *Ladies Home Journal*. The *Police Gazette* and other men's magazines were eye-opening to a young school boy.

My folks drove a Model A Ford they had bought from

14

"Daa," my grandmother Nannie Ernestine George. Even in the late 1940s, the old Ford was badly out of style, all squarish and black with wire wheels. The roof leaked, and Daddy had to patch it with tar. In wet weather, the engine wiring would get damp, and Daddy would raise the sheet metal side curtains on the engine and hold burning newspapers up near the spark plug wires to dry them out. One time when Daddy was drying out the wires, I ran out of the garage yelling, "Fire! Fire!" Boy, did I get a talking to! But even with its problems, we were glad to have the old Ford.

Larry learned to drive the Model A on Hunt County dirt roads while he was sitting on the folded-down front seat. He did fine too, until he came to a "T" intersection south of Commerce. Mom couldn't get to the brake because of Larry and the folded seat, and we went through the intersection and then turned abruptly to the right. The car came to a stop with its left side resting against the far ditch bank. Mom got Larry out of the front seat, put the old Ford back in gear, and drove right out of the ditch. That was the end of Larry's driving lesson for the day. Because I was younger, I never got any driving lessons in the Model A Ford. I wish I had.

During the winter, one of Mom's favorite activities was reading through seed catalogs in preparation for a spring garden. Mom first taught me about plants by placing dry lima beans in a glass jar and holding them against the sides with wet blotting paper. As the beans sprouted, we could see the roots, stem, and leaves as they developed. I suspect this was something she had learned as a school teacher.

We also raised sweet potato slips by placing a whole sweet potato upright in a jar of water. As the roots sprouted and grew downward into the water, green stems and leaves grew out of the top of the sweet potato. When the tops grew into vines several feet long, the vines could be cut into sections called slips and planted in the garden outdoors. If you didn't want to plant the slips in the garden, the sprouted sweet potato made a nice house plant.

Daddy had raised pet rabbits when he was a boy so he thought we should have some too. He built us a good rabbit hutch and got Larry and me a couple of rabbits. Larry's was black, and he called her "Blacky." Mine was black and white spotted, so I called her "Whitey." I was apparently name-challenged at the time. Over the years, we raised several litters of baby rabbits. There is hardly anything cuter than a baby rabbit. We later had registered New Zealand Red rabbits we bought from a Mr. Perkins who worked with Daddy on the railroad. We named our first red rabbit "Perky" in his honor.

A lot of boys I knew had a bug jar they used to capture insects. The bug jar was usually a glass fruit jar with holes punched in the metal lid so that the bugs could breath. We

Ronnie and Larry with pet rabbits, 1953. Note Ronnie's safety patrol uniform. —Photo by Dorris George

would catch butterflies, bees, and wasps during the day and lightning bugs (fireflies) at night. After we played with them a while, we usually turned them loose. Once when we were on summer vacation in Arkansas, Larry and I filled up a bug jar with grasshoppers for fish bait, but we forgot them. A couple of days later while we were still on the road, a faint but hideous odor began to waft through the car. After several hours, the odor got much stronger, and we finally realized it was coming from our bug jar under Mom's front seat. Mom was not pleased!

One day, Larry and I found a large insect cocoon made of spun silk in a mulberry tree in our backyard. We brought the cocoon into the house, and Mom carefully pinned it to the wallpaper near a window. In a few days, the cocoon hatched, and a beautiful brown, red, and cream-colored cecropia moth with a wingspan of nearly 6 inches emerged, slowly dried its wings, and flew to the window screen. Our moth must have been a female exuding sex pheromones because that night there were more than a dozen cecropia moths clinging to the outside of our window screen. It was an impressive sight.

When I was in the sixth grade at A. L. Day Elementary School, the school sponsored a magazine sales program for the students. I think the school received some free books and magazines, and the students learned about salesmanship. In exchange for selling magazine subscriptions, students were allowed to select prizes from a catalog depending upon how many sales they made. I found it was not easy to go door to door and try to sell something to strangers. However, after approaching enough people who knew me or my folks, I sold enough magazine subscriptions to receive a small, cheap hunting knife as a prize. I still have that rusty knife to remind me of my early days as a salesman.

Girls were always something of a mystery to me since I didn't have any sisters. However, one day at recess when I was still in the fourth grade, Martha Allard, the prettiest girl in class, suddenly ran her fingers through my curly blond hair and said to her girlfriend, Ronda Myers, who was standing near by, "This is what I like about him." Well, until that moment, I had never really liked my curly hair. It was hard to comb, and no one else in my class had hair like that. After Martha's reaction, however, I decided curly hair might not be so bad after all!

Sometime later, I recall telling Martha about a tadpole that Larry and I found while seining a mudpuddle with a sheet of screen wire. The tadpole was just turning into a frog. It still had a tail, but it also had four legs. Martha seemed to be fascinated with my story. She said, "If you will bring me a four-legged tadpole, I will love you forever." Although I looked hard, I never found another four-legged tadpole to give her. Martha died of an enlarged heart when we were in the sixthth grade. I knew old people passed away, but I didn't know that happened to pretty young girls.

The Cotton Belt Roundhouse

"Oh, I've been working on the railroad,
All the livelong day,
I've been working on the railroad,
Just to pass the time away,
Don't you hear that whistle blowing?
Rise up so early in the morn.
I'll be working on the railroad –
'Til Gabriel blows his horn."
　　　　　—American folk song from the 1890s

During the 1940s and '50s, Commerce, Texas, was a railroad town, and my daddy was a railroader, a fireman, on the Cotton Belt Railroad (the Saint Louis Southwestern). I recall lying awake at night listening to the ghostly whistle of big steam engines and hearing the windows of our house on Locust Street rattle when a train rolled down the tracks a quarter mile away. Steam engines that shook the ground, boxcars, cabooses, the call boy, train orders, train order string, the passenger train station, the freight office, and the roundhouse were a big part of my early life in Commerce.

Commerce is located about halfway between Texarkana and Fort Worth, about a 100 miles either way. At the time the railroad was built, 100 miles was a standard daily trip for a steam engine. Commerce had a roundhouse, repair shops, fuel and water tanks, a railroad pool, and all of the other things needed to operate steam engines.

My daddy, Cotton Belt fireman Cecil George (right) and engineer D. M. Newton with a new diesel engine at Commerce, Texas, early 1950s. Daddy is still wearing his steam engine "uniform" of overalls and railroader's cap. The engineer has already switched to "civies" that could be worn with the cleaner diesels. —Photo courtesy of Commerce Public Library

The roundhouse was a massive structure of yellowish-brown bricks and dark wooden beams that smelled of engine smoke and creosote. It was big enough to house several steam engines. The roundhouse was built as a series of long triangular bays or stalls which curved in a semicircle around a pit which held the turntable. Between the tracks in each bay was a recessed concrete pit where workmen could stand and work under an engine. The exposed framework of beams that supported the roundhouse roof was blackened by decades of train smoke. Pigeons roosted and nested on the beams and flew in and out through the huge open doors. When a train whistled, and the smoke rolled up, and the engine started to move out of the roundhouse, the pigeons would scatter in panic only to return when the train was gone.

The high ceiling of the roundhouse made for a cool place on a hot summer day, and I usually jumped at a

Cotton Belt roundhouse and turntable at Commerce, Texas, during steam engine days.

—Photo courtesy of Commerce Public Library

chance to go with Daddy down to the roundhouse to "check the board." The board was a blackboard marked with wet chalk to show the schedule for trains and train crews. Crewmembers bid on jobs and were assigned to crews based on seniority. The board was constantly changing as trains and crews came and went. By checking the board, crews had a general idea of when they would go to work, but nothing was certain until Pat Patterson, the "call boy," made the official telephone call. I recall once when the call boy came to the house to call Daddy because a storm had knocked out the telephone lines.

The roundhouse had the first cold water drinking fountain I ever remember. Daddy would hold me up to the fountain so I could get a drink, or he would hand me a little folded white paper cup he had filled with delicious cold water.

There was a smaller brick building off to the left as you entered the roundhouse. That building housed the air compressor. The compressed air was used to test air brake lines on the trains, power huge grease guns, and run the turntable. The air compressor was not operated all of the time, but it was an awesome sight when it was running. The compressor had a vertically-mounted, weighted flywheel that must have been 10 feet in diameter. About half the flywheel was in a pit below the floor, and there were belts and pulleys, and a governor to control the speed of the machine. The governor consisted of two red-painted steel balls about the size of grapefruit that rocked back and forth on short arms. When it was running, and the flywheel was going round and round, and the governor was clicking back and forth, and the compressor was a going "auf ah chuffa," "auf ah chuffa," like a gigantic bicycle pump, it was hard to imagine anything short of a steam locomotive that could be more powerful. Years later, I saw a steam-powered air compressor like the one at Commerce in the Smithsonian Museum in Washington, D.C.

Sometimes after Daddy had checked the board, he would take Larry and me over to one of the big steam engines standing silently in the roundhouse, and we would get to climb up into the cab. This was in the days before OSHA (Occupational Safety and Hazard Act), but Daddy wisely only did this when there were no railroad "bigshots" (company officials) around.

One day when I was about six years old, my cousin Bobby Ridley was visiting, and Daddy took Bobby, Larry, and me to the roundhouse. On this occasion, Daddy needed to get a steam engine started and serviced for a run. He led us in a walk-around inspection of the engine (much like I did with airplanes in later years). Daddy then let us crawl up the ladder into the cab. To start the engine, I recall Daddy opened the firebox door and picked up a big wad of textile-mill threads called "waste." He held the waste in his left hand and squirted several squirts of engine oil from a

Number 679, the last Cotton Belt steam engine to pull a passenger train from Commerce to Dallas, early 1950s.
—Photo courtesy of Commerce Public Library

long-spouted railroad oilcan onto the waste. He took a wooden kitchen match, struck it on the firewall at the front of the cab, and lit the waste. Then he turned a valve on the fuel line and threw the burning waste way back in the firebox. There was a loud "whoosh" sound, and in a short time there was a fire roaring in the firebox. After several minutes, the engine had built up enough steam to move.

Daddy blew the whistle, the pigeons scattered, and Daddy backed the engine out of the roundhouse and onto the turntable. He stopped the train, set the brakes, left us in the cab, and stepped down to operate the turntable. The table moved ponderously around, and eventually we stopped with the engine headed west toward the main line to Dallas. Daddy climbed back into the cab and moved us slowly down to the water tank where he stopped the train, let the three of us off, and sent us over to the car where Mom was waiting for us.

To old railroad hands like Larry and me, this was interesting, but not too unusual, but to Bobby, the son of a Methodist minister, this must have seemed like the adventure of a lifetime. Decades later, he still talks about that day at the roundhouse.

The railroad pool, where they got water for the steam engines, was another interesting spot near the roundhouse. On summer evenings when Daddy was going out on a run, he often would drive the family to the roundhouse, and Mom would sit in the car and read for an hour or so while Daddy prepared the engine. Once the train was ready, Daddy would park it by the water tank, come over to the car, kiss Mom goodbye, and swing back up into the cab. For Larry and me, that hour or so parked by the roundhouse was a time of high adventure. Our excursions often took us down to the Railroad Pool. The pool, and its feeder ditches, was a wonderful place full of oozing mud, stinking water, willow trees, cattails, frogs, turtles, and red-winged blackbird nests. I got some of my earliest appreciation for wildlife at the Railroad Pool.

One day in the late 1940s, Daddy came home from a trip telling about a new kind of railroad engine he had seen in Texarkana. He said this thing was painted purple, and it was called a "diesel." I couldn't wait to see a purple diesel. I didn't realize at the time that the more efficient diesel-electric engines would ultimately mean the end of steam engines, the roundhouse, the turntable, the air compressor, and all the rest. Only the main line and the Railroad Pool remain at Commerce today.

Toy Trains

"I hope Santa Claus brings us an electric train."
—My brother Larry, late 1940s

Larry and I grew up in a railroad family, and I guess it was just natural for us to want an electric train for Christmas. I couldn't understand why Santa Claus wouldn't bring us one. Mom said Santa probably thought they were just too expensive. Several years later when I finally saw the price of a Lionel electric train in the Sears and Roebuck Catalogue, I began to understand.

Since a store-bought train set seemed unlikely, Larry and I decided to make our own. Larry was a great one for precision. He insisted all of our locomotives and train cars meet certain standards. As I recall, we made all of our "rolling stock" out of 2" x 2" pine boards cut exactly eight inches long. The diesel engines had a neat cutout on the front to represent the cab and the hood. We sanded all of the corners and carefully hand-painted the engines a glossy black with a bright red stripe along the side just like the real engines we saw down at the Commerce railroad station. Our engines and cars were coupled together with screw-in "eyes" and "hooks" we bought at the hardware store.

Our tracks and landscape were drawn in Crayola crayon on an 8' x 12' sheet of rolled-up cardboard we got from the furniture store. On rainy days, we would unroll our cardboard on the big, covered front porch on Ash Street, carefully arrange our trains, cars, and buildings, and play with our trains for hours.

One day, Larry and I were supposed to be watching Mike who was pushing himself around on the porch in his stroller. While we were busy with our train set, Mike drove his stroller off the porch and down the three wooden steps to the concrete sidewalk below. Fortunately, he landed on his hard head and wasn't seriously hurt. But we were in trouble again!

Larry, of course, was always upgrading the train set by adding more cars, buildings, bridges, and the like. I thought one of his best additions was the water tower. The water tower was made from a two-pound Folgers coffee can mounted on a little wooden stand. To make it more serviceable, Larry punched a small hole in the bottom of the can and ran a tiny rubber tube down to a bottle cork which represented a rain barrel by the train station. By inserting a straight pin in the end of rubber tube, Larry could cap the tiny drinking fountain on the barrel when we weren't using it. It was pretty impressive.

We kept the train set for several years and played with it lots of times. With all of the cheap plastic toys available to children today, I have often wondered if they wouldn't be better off making their own toys like we did.

Train Wrecks

"Well, the Caller called Casey at half past four.
He kissed his wife at the station door.
He mounted to the cabin with the orders in his hand,
and he took his farewell trip to the Promised Land."

—"Casey Jones," American folk song
from the early 1900s.

Larry and I often sang along with the Casey Jones song when we played it on our 78 rpm record player, but I didn't really understand what it was all about until Daddy took Larry and me out one night to the old, seldom-used, Sherman Branch railroad tracks north of Commerce. As we were standing by the tracks in the dark, Daddy began telling us a story about a Tennessee railroad engineer named Casey Jones. Daddy said Casey was pouring the coals to his steam locomotive one night, trying to make up time, when he saw a red warning flare on the tracks ahead. Daddy then reached into his pocket and took out something that looked like a ten-inch long stick of dynamite. Daddy said it was called a "fusee." Daddy quickly removed the cap from the fusee, exposed the scratch mix, and struck it on the ignitor. There was a hissing sound, and the night was

28

filled with a bright red light and billowing white smoke as the fusee ignited.

Daddy dropped the fusee on the tracks and said Casey Jones had seen a similar red warning flare on his tracks that night long ago but failed to stop his train, apparently thinking the signal was a mistake or a prank. As Casey's train rounded the next bend, however, he saw the red tail lights of a caboose and a string of boxcars stalled on the tracks ahead of him. Casey told his fireman "Jump!" Casey could have jumped too, but he made a heroic effort to stop his train. Daddy said Casey died with one hand on the brake lever and one on the whistle cord. The popular Casey Jones song we sung so happily was really about a deadly train wreck.

Some time later, I recall going down to the Cotton Belt Train Station in Commerce to watch Daddy bring in a work train dragging the aftermath of a train wreck. Daddy had been gone for several days with the work train over toward Dallas while they cleaned up a derailment. The train came into the yard slowly like a funeral procession. Gawkers lined the tracks. Nearly every car showed damage. Several boxcars had their sides caved in. Some cars showed signs of lying on their sides or tops in the grass, gravel, and mud. Some of the cars were chained together. It looked like a moving battlefield. Toward the end of the train was a massive wrecker, as big as a locomotive. Behind the wrecker was a caboose, and finally, a boxcar with a good coupling only on the front end; the rear coupling was snapped off like a match stick. It was hard for me to imagine the forces that had caused all of this damage, but I suddenly had a better understanding of the dangers Daddy faced daily in providing for his family.

During the 1950s, there were several fatal accidents on the Cotton Belt. Several times after my folks thought I was asleep, I recall hearing Daddy telling Mom about a serious accident which had just happened. Once, the side of his train had been struck at night at a road crossing by a car-load of teenage boys who were all killed in the collision. As I recall, that was the first time I had ever heard Daddy cry. He was telling Mom he could just imagine those boys asking their Daddy if it would be all right for them to use the car that night.

I also recall going to a home in Greenville with Daddy so he could pay his condolences to the family of a young man who he had helped get a job as a fireman on the Cotton Belt. The young fireman was in the cab of a locomotive moving smoothly down the tracks when he saw a gasoline truck coming up fast on the right side at the next road crossing. In desperation, the young man jumped out the left side of the cab only to be caught in the flames as the truck hit the front of the engine, swung around on the left side, and exploded.

Another accident involving a gasoline truck claimed the lives of another train crew Daddy knew, and he had a terrible premonition the same thing was going to happen to him. Fortunately, he was able to retire after twenty-eight years with the Cotton Belt. Unfortunately, one of the crews he had been working with were all killed when they hit a gasoline truck just two weeks after he retired.

During the late 1990s after Mom and Daddy passed way, I was cleaning out their farm house when I came across copies of some of Daddy's signed accident reports. As I read those yellowed pages, one dated August 8, 1956, gave me a chill. Daddy's report said, "Our train consisted of a 3-Unit Diesel, and we were handling 67-15-3228 tons. As our engine approached the Hager Switch Crossing, I was back in the second unit checking the equipment. From my position in the unit, I could not see the crossing, but I could hear the engineer sounding the regulation crossing whistle. The first knowledge I had that something was wrong was when I heard the air go into emergency. We were moving at a speed of about forty MPH. I could tell the engineer had started sounding the horn, and I quickly began to brace myself in the unit. After the impact, the train stopped twenty-two car lengths past the crossing. The brakeman then came up and said we had hit a truck carrying a dragline." Daddy's report didn't say what happened to the truck driver.

Campbell Stories

"Bees won't sting you at night
because they can't see you"
—My daddy, Cecil George, c. 1953

Both of my parents grew to adulthood in Campbell, Texas, and my Grandmother George (Daa) and my Grandfather Ridley (Paw Paw) still lived in nice houses in Campbell during the late 1940s and early '50s. Larry, Mike, and I spent a lot of time in Campbell as we were growing up. Both of our folks were from big families, and the Georges and the Ridleys had great family reunions with lots of visiting with aunts, uncles, and cousins, and lots of good things to eat. The gardens, cow pastures, and fields at both of my grandparents' places were great places for grandchildren to play.

My Uncle Bob Ridley had a beautiful log cabin that he had built next to Paw Paw's house. The cabin had fireplaces, wood paneling, a pump organ, and the wonderful smell of cedar shingles, wood smoke, and old books.

My cousin, Angela Cole, had a girl's bicycle that I learned to ride on a two-rut, dirt lane in Campbell. I recall trying to balance on the bicycle seat without moving forward so that it wouldn't hurt so much when I fell off. No one told me that it is actually easier to ride a bike when it is moving forward and the gyroscopic force of the turning wheels helps hold the bike upright.

Larry had just gotten a new Daisy pump-action BB gun for his birthday, and we were playing out in the back lot at Daa's place. We had already murdered several tin cans, a fruit jar we were not supposed to shoot, and few grasshoppers, but we were now looking for bigger game. We knew we were not supposed to be shooting at the chickens or breaking eggs, but we thought there might be something else we could get into in Daa's barn. The barn was really just a long series of sheds under one roof where my grandmother stored chicken feed, tools, and old stuff she no longer needed.

The rusty hinges screeched as we opened the wooden door to the first shed. We pushed the cobwebs aside and crawled up into the darkened room. We could see old bed springs leaning against the far wall, a few rusty garden tools, boxes of old newspapers and magazines out in the middle, and an old chest of drawers against the east wall of the room. The walls of each room didn't go all the way to the ceiling but stopped about eight feet up so that air could circulate from one room to the next. After checking out other things in the room, our interest centered upon the old chest of drawers. What treasures did it hold? As we pulled open the top drawer, almost into our faces, we realized that the drawer was packed level—full with live rats!

For a second or more, no one moved. The rats just silently watched us with their beady eyes. Then, in one motion, a solid mass of gray rats erupted out of the drawer and flowed like a living curtain over the top of the chest, up the wall, and over into the next room. When we recovered from the shock, we ran next door, but the room was empty! We spent the rest of the afternoon hunting rats but only found one.

That evening, Larry prepared a very realistic Crayola drawing of 100 or more rats going up a wall. He took his drawing to school the next day and told his story to his class, but even with his great drawing, no one could really believe a "living curtain of rats." You would've had to have been there!

Another Campbell adventure began when Larry and I and several of our Ridley cousins were exploring some fields behind Paw Paw's house one Sunday afternoon. As we were walking along the edge of a cottonfield, we discovered a big swarm of honey bees hanging just a few feet off the ground in a box elder tree in the fencerow. I am not sure why we didn't just chunk some dirt clods at the bees, but we reported our find to the folks back at Paw Paw's house. Daddy said it would be nice to have a hive of honey bees and that we ought to capture the swarm and put 'em in a hive.

Some of Daddy's railroad buddies (always a great source of knowledge) had told him that bees couldn't see at night, and that you could handle bees at night without getting stung because they couldn't see you. We didn't have a wooden beehive on hand, but Daddy thought we could put the swarm in a cardboard box and later transfer them to a hive.

Well, Daddy woke Larry and me up in the middle of the night, and we drove back to Campbell to box the swarm of bees. Larry's job was to hold the box under the swarm, my job was to hold the flashlight, and Daddy planned to take a long-handled clothes brush and gently brush the bees off the limb and into the box. It didn't work out quite that way. As soon as Daddy's brush touched the swarm, the bees begin to sting him on the hands and arms, and some of the bees begin to fly toward the flashlight I was holding. One bee stung me on the wrist, and others were buzzing in my hair as I deserted my post and ran off into the cottonfield leaving Daddy and Larry in the dark! About that time, Daddy and Larry decided this wasn't working very well, and they deserted their posts too! In later years, we raised a bunch of bees at the farm, but we never again attempted to work them in the dark as we had at the "Campbell bee boxing."

Greenville Schools

"Let's have three cheers
for the boys who brew the beer
in the cellars of old Junior High.
And if Baker comes down here,
we'll say, 'Baker, Have a beer.'
In the cellars of old Junior High."
—Greenville Junior High song, c. 1955

In September 1955, I began an exciting new chapter in my life when I met the students and teachers of my new seventh grade class at Greenville Junior High School. Since I had transferred in from Commerce, all of the faces were new to me. They were a great bunch of kids. Most of the boys wore blue jeans and had short haircuts. A few of the tough guys wore leather jackets and ducktails. The girls wore neat dresses or skirts. White bobbie socks and penny loafers were popular. There were hundreds of students and a lot of activity in Greenville Junior High.

The Junior High building was a large, three-story, dark-brick structure with tall metal fire escape slides running up both sides of the building. The rooms and grounds at Junior High were crowded. Several classes were taught in one-story "temporary" buildings out back. During class

36

changes, locker doors slammed and voices echoed through the buildings. Teachers stood by in the halls to monitor student behavior.

School teachers in those days enjoyed a lot of respect. They were often some of the best-educated people in town and were frequently leaders in their community and church as well. Students generally did what their teachers told them to do. If they didn't, the teacher contacted their parents.

One of the most effective and memorable teachers I ever met was Mr. Keith Bearden. He was my bus driver and seventh grade teacher (and later my ninth grade science teacher). Mr. Bearden was a young, bright, handsome U.S. Army veteran who had served with the field artillery in Europe during the last fifteen months of World War II. He was a great role model for his students.

Mr. Bearden reached out to all of his students, offering them guidance, advice, hope, encouragement, and leadership by example. He told great stories. He knew when to joke and when to be serious. He was always saying things like, "Just as sure as God made little green apples, and he made 'em too, didn't he, Jerry?, we are going to have a test on Friday" (Jerry Mainord was a likeable and popular class leader who later became a U.S. Army lieutenant colonel). Mr. Bearden would help us out though and let us know what was really important (and likely to be on the test) by stomping on the wooden floor three times. We quickly got the message.

One of the most serious threats a teacher like Mr. Bearden could make if a student was acting up would be to say, "Lloyd, meet me in the Boiler Room" (Lloyd Suggs was a funny, smart, athletic, and often-mischievous student.) The Boiler Room was in the basement (the cellar) of the building. This was where paddlings were sometimes administered. We didn't even like to think about being sent to see Mr. Baker, the Junior High School principal.

At lunch time, Junior High kids had the option of eating in the school cafeteria (Ptomaine City) or at the Malt Burger, Sabine Valley Ice Cream Store, Ernie's Barbecue, Paul's Café, CB's Hamburger or a number of lunch counters downtown. At noon one day, I was with a bunch of the guys headed south down Wesley Street toward CB's when we came to a freight train completely blocking Wesley. Some of the guys swung up on the boxcar ladders, stepped over the train couplings between the boxcars, and jumped down on the other side. Everything was going smoothly until the train started to move. Some of the latecomers were carried quite a ways down the track as they struggled to get between the boxcars and jump clear on the other side. A concerned citizen reported this incident to Mr. Bearden, and we were in trouble again! Mr. Bearden rounded up the usual suspects and told us we should have been smarter than that.

The next year, we met Miss Camp, our eighth grade science teacher. Miss Camp was a small, elderly, white-haired woman who didn't put up with any nonsense in her classroom. One day, Miss Camp was explaining the chemical wonders of the Periodic Table when she noticed Freddy Bennett was looking out the windows at the back of the room. (Freddy was a friendly, talkative guy with an inquisitive mind who later became a U.S. Air Force captain, communications officer, and missile commander). Miss Camp barked, "Freddy!" and he returned his attention to the classroom. In just a little bit, however, Freddy was looking out the window again. Miss Camp went charging back there to straighten him out, but Freddy just pointed out the window and said, "Shouldn't we be doing something about that?" Miss Camp took one glance at the boiling green sky and said, "Oh my gracious!" She ran out of the room, and we soon heard Mr. Baker's voice on the squawk box directing everyone to move quickly and quietly to the basement of the building. The storm passed without causing much damage, but you never know with a Texas tornado. After that, Miss Camp never again said anything to Freddy about looking out the window.

As we moved on to Greenville High School, our class was always into something. When we were seniors, everyone brought marbles to school one day, and we took them to the auditorium for "assembly." Wayne Little, our Student Body President, was standing at the podium giving a presentation when he casually touched a finger to his ear. This was the secret signal for all the seniors to drop their marbles on the concrete floor. There was stunned silence in the big room as hundreds of glass marbles rolled, clattered, and echoed down to the front of the stage. Our unofficial class motto the year we graduated from Greenville High School was, "Mean as hell, full of fun, we're the class of '61."

Lloyd Suggs and several of our classmates are now gone but not forgotten, but I still see Wayne Little, Jerry Mainord, and many of our other classmates at Greenville High School reunions. Mr. Bearden (now Dr. Bearden) still lives in the Greenville area and often attends our reunions. Our reunions are always noisy and exciting, just like that seventh grade class from long ago. We are still looking for trouble!

The Farm on Timber Creek

"When bois d'arc leaves are the size of possum ears,
it is time to plant cotton."
—Mr. Keith Bearden
Bus driver and
seventh grade teacher

The George Family Farm is located east of Greenville in the Shady Grove Community of Northeast Texas. The farm straddles the transition from Blackland Prairie to Post Oak Savannah. Timber Creek, a tributary of the Sabine River, meanders across the south end of the property. The farm is the home of mockingbirds, cardinals, cottontails, jack rabbits, armadillos, green racers, chicken snakes, great horned owls, and many other species of wildlife. My daddy loved the farm and taught me the names of most of the wild animals and plants.

Although my folks left the farm before I was born and moved to Commerce so Daddy could work on the railroad during the War, they kept the family farm on Timber Creek. It was usually an adventure to go down to the farm.

I picked my first and last cotton on the same day at that farm when I was five years old. As a boy, my daddy had spent a lot of time picking cotton at Van and Campbell.

Times were very hard then, and some years Daddy had to stay out of school until nearly Christmas picking cotton to help support his family. Daddy apparently thought it would be a good idea for his sons to see what cotton picking was all about. Mom made me a little cotton sack out of a pillow case with a cloth shoulder strap. Larry was already in school at the time and escaped this educational opportunity.

Daddy had a sharecropper by the name of Mr. Horton who lived in the old farmhouse and raised cotton in the big field. At Daddy's request, Mr. Horton showed me how to quickly and carefully pull the cotton lint and attached seed out of each woody boll and put it into my cotton sack. We actually picked cotton that day and didn't "pull bolls" as pickers were able to do a few years later when cotton ginning equipment was improved. Cotton bolls are stickery at the open end and hard on your hands. After some time, I was able to fill up my pillow-case cotton sack and drag it to the scale hanging in the old Chinaberry tree in the front yard of the farmhouse. Mr. Horton carefully weighed my cotton and paid me 35 cents (a quarter and a dime) for my work. This was probably the first money I ever earned. I suspect I was overpaid.

Daddy had performed hard physical labor much of his life, and despite his long hours on the railroad, he apparently felt the continued need for physical exertion. Anyhow, when I was about five, we went down to the farm, and Daddy started to clear a "boardark" (bois d'arc) hedgerow about twenty feet wide and about a half mile long with an axe. His axe was a beautiful, shiny, double-bitted thing he lovingly sharpened with a file before each outing and as needed during the day. Daddy was really careful with his tools.

Larry and I were still too small to drag brush, but when we were not in school, we got to go to the farm. While Daddy cut brush, we wandered all over the two hundred-acre farm. Larry and I went wading, chased bugs, frogs, and snakes, shot Larry's BB gun, and stole our first watermelon from the Mr. Horton's patch. We could always find some kind of trouble to get into.

In 1955, when I was twelve years old, my folks built a new house and moved back to the farm on Timber Creek. Although I had visited the farm many times when I was growing up, and Daddy had often talked of moving back to the farm, I thought it was just wishful thinking. However, in the spring of '55, my folks contracted with Anderson Lumber Company of Greenville to build a six-room, red-wood and Austin stone, ranch-style house within ninety days. Existing records indicate my folks paid $11,040 cash for the house and borrowed $5,000 to pay for the water well, pumphouse, dirt work, and other improvements.

Daddy wanted the house to be built in a grove of post oak trees so he hired a man with a gasoline-powered circular saw mounted flat on a little 2-wheel cart to cut the pole-sized trees in the grove where the house would go. This was in the days before chain saws were in common use. Once the trees were cut, Daddy took Larry and me down to the farm one night. Daddy showed us how to use a flash light and some reflective tape to carefully set foundation stakes among the stumps so the house would be lined up with the North Star. Daddy didn't want a house that wasn't set right with the world.

The summer the house was being built, Daddy, Larry, and I spent a lot of time at the farm, and I got my first glimpse of what farm work was going to be like. As I recall, we dragged a lot of post oak limbs, piled a lot of brush, and later picked up endless tree roots in a three-acre spot south of the house Daddy had selected for a garden and orchard.

Farm Animals

"Can you wiggle your fingers?"
"You didn't break your arm."
—My brother Larry, c. 1957

In September 1955, we moved into the new house at the farm. Our first morning there, I recall waking up to the sounds of Mr. Pitt's cows across the fence. That certainly sounded promising to a new farm boy!

I had saved $20 out of my quarter per week allowance to buy a black heifer calf, and Paw Paw Ridley said he would find me one. I was imagining a two-week-old calf, but Paw Paw bought a five-month old calf that weighed about 175 pounds. The calf cost $34.35. Paw Paw said I could pay him the rest when I got the money.

I had already decided I was going to call the new calf "Bessie." So when Larry and I got in from school, we went up to the barn to see Bessie. The cattle trader who delivered Bessie had put her in the milk stall, and it was Larry's and my task to put a rope on her and lead her to the Little Pool for a drink. We were concerned she might be a little wild, and we were smart enough not to open the outside door. However, when we went around and opened the door to the feed room, Bessie promptly jumped up into the feed room and almost jumped out of the front door of the barn which was about four feet off the ground. We eventually got Bessie back down into the stall and got a six-foot lead rope tied to her leather halter. She would not lead out of the stall with both of us pulling on the rope. So Larry held the rope, and I went back around to drive her out. Bessie shot out the door, jerked Larry to the ground, and dragged him across the cow lot. Fortunately, Larry didn't let go, and Bessie eventually stopped with a wild look in her eyes. We somehow got her back in the stall, carried her a bucket of water, and waited for Daddy to come home and share some advice on watering wild stock.

Daddy said Bessie was just scared of us and that a longer rope should do the trick. Daddy got me a hundred feet of one-inch rope, and sure enough, Larry and I together could just about manage to water Bessie and tie her out so she could graze. We had to keep Bessie staked out because none of the old rusty fences on the farm would hold her.

The only problem with this arrangement was that Larry soon tired of helping water my livestock, and I had to do it by myself. Bessie and I eventually worked out a system. I would go to where she was staked out, drive her around to where she was between me and the Little Pool, untie her rope, and drive her to water and back. As long as I stayed at my end of the hundred-foot rope, Bessie was OK, but I wanted to gentle her down. So each day while she was still staked out, I would talk quietly to her and work my way up the rope toward her until she would bolt, jerk the rope out of my hands, and run off in an arc at the end of the rope. One day, I got nearly up to where I could pet her before she ran. This time, however, instead of running away from me to the right and jerking the rope out of my hands, she ran to the left. The rope caught me across the chest and throat and knocked me backward to the ground. I hit the back of my head hard, saw stars, and was knocked unconscious.

When I came to, I was lying on my back, and Bessie was looking at me from the far end of the rope.

Paw Paw knew what a struggle I was having with Bessie, so he offered to take her down to the Ridley Homeplace where he had some cows on a harvested oat field. I said that sounded pretty good to me so we loaded Bessie in the stock trailer and took her to the Homeplace south of Campbell. As we were unloading Bessie, I recall telling Paw Paw we had better tie the hundred-foot rope back on to the six-foot lead rope so we could handle her. Paw Paw gently told me he didn't think that would be necessary, and with that, he opened the trailer and lead Bessie out. Wild Young Bessie saw the other cows and went past

Ronnie and Mike with their show calves, c. 1960.
—Photo by Dorris George

Paw Paw like a bullet, but instead of jerking Paw Paw down, he jerked her down, like a calf in a rodeo, with only one hand on the rope. Bessie didn't know it, but besides being a stockman most of his life, Paw Paw also had been one of the earliest college football players in Texas. Even though he was about seventy years old at the time, he was still a big, powerful man! I was certainly impressed, and I suspect Bessie was too because she just stood there while Paw Paw walked up to her, removed the leather halter, and freed her with the rest of the cows.

With Bessie gone, we got quite a bit of fencing done, and several months later, we were ready to bring Bessie back home. When we went to pick her up, I hardly recognized her. Bessie was now a sleek, fat, responsible cow who became the first of five animals in my cowherd. The herd ultimately included "Droopy," a tall, aloof Brahman cow with droopy ears and "Dixie Belle," my blocky, little registered Black Angus heifer that won Grand Champion Angus Female at the Hunt County Junior Livestock Show in 1959. Those cows helped put me through college.

Shorty was a little Banty (Bantam) rooster a lady in Commerce had given us. Shorty looked like a small version of a red jungle fowl, the wild ancestor of all domestic chickens. He had a full red comb, orange neck feathers, iridescent greenish-black body and tail feathers, and feathered legs, like bell-bottom trousers. Like all Banty roosters, Shorty was very proud of himself and convinced of his own importance. When Shorty would crow, he would throw his head forward so hard he would lift himself off the ground. We all enjoyed hearing Shorty crow early in the morning.

Right after we moved to the farm, we got Shorty several little Banty hens for company. One of the hens was all black, like "Higgledy Piggledy." We only thought Shorty had been strutting before! Now, he could really put on a show for his harem. In no time at all, we were getting fresh eggs every morning. The hens laid eggs all over the place—in the hen house, out in the weeds, up in the loft, and under the barn. The trick was to find the nests while the eggs where still fresh; otherwise we would have a setting hen and a bunch of new chicks.

We had a constant battle, however, with possums, polecats, and other varmints catching the chickens and eating eggs. One evening just about sundown, I crawled under the barn to gather some eggs. It was already getting pretty dark under the barn, but I knew where the hens had been laying, so I just wriggled over to one of the nests. I was expecting to see the gleam of white eggs, but I didn't see anything but blackness. After a second or two, my eyes adjusted to the darkness, and I realized the eggs were completely covered by a huge black snake just inches from my face! I jerked back and hit my head on the floor of the barn! After I got out from under the barn and recovered from the shock, I realized it was just a harmless chicken snake (Texas rat snake) which had been eating the eggs. I crawled back under the barn, the snake was gone, and I gathered the remaining eggs.

Some time later, I was shoveling last-year's cotton seed hulls out of a crib in the barn when I disturbed a rat that had been hiding in the hulls. As the rat ran toward a darkened corner of the crib, a big chicken snake that was hidden in the darkness suddenly looped a couple of coils around the rat's body. I didn't disturb the snake but continued shoveling. Pretty soon, a second rat shot off in the same direction only to be snared in the coils of the snake. I didn't know a chicken snake could catch two rats at once. I figured the snake was just paying for the eggs he ate.

A year or so after Shorty passed on to the big chicken house in the sky, someone gave us a Crowned Polish rooster we called "Morgen" (the German word for "morning"). Morgen was all black except for a crown of white feathers which drooped down over his eyes like an English sheep-dog. As he got older, Morgen got pretty feisty and would run all the way across the barn lot to chase my little brother Mike. Daddy thought it was pretty funny until he was bending over picking up a sack of feed in the barn door and Morgen came up behind him and raked him with his spurs. Daddy whirled around, and Morgen came at him again. Daddy jerked a pair of heavy wirecutters out of his overall pocket and whacked Morgen across the head. Morgen was invited to Sunday dinner.

Shortly after we moved to the farm, my folks said that if we worked hard and helped out a lot, they would get us a horse to ride. Sure enough, several months later Paw Paw located a tall, stylish-looking, black and white paint mare with four white stocking feet. We called her "Lindy" after the previous owner's wife, Linda. (I am sure she would have been honored.) Lindy was a pretty good old horse for a bunch of kids. She was a little long in the tooth, a little sway-backed, a little jumpy, and a little hard to catch, but once we got ahold of her, she would carry kids double or even triple, and we could ride her bareback by holding on to her mane.

I recall one day, though, when Larry thought he would improve Lindy's looks by trimming her mane. It changed her looks all right—she looked like a mule! But the worst thing about the haircut was we no longer had a mane to hold on to. We could have put a saddle on Lindy, but that was a lot of work, so we rode sorta balanced on her back.

One day, I was riding down through the pasture to get the cows at a pretty good clip through knee-high weeds when we passed a pile of posts. Old Lindy must have seen a booger because she suddenly jumped sideways out from under me. I went flying and landed on my left arm. It hurt so much I figured I had probably broken it, but I caught Lindy and led her back up to the barn where Larry was milking the cow. I told Larry, "I fell off the horse and broke my arm." He said, "Can you wiggle your fingers?" Well, I tried it and showed Larry I could, and Larry said, "You didn't break your arm." So I turned Lindy loose and walked back to the house where I went in the kitchen and told Mom, "I fell off the horse and broke my arm." She said, "Can you wiggle your fingers?" I showed her I could, and she said, "You didn't break your arm." Well, about ten days later, we were at a family reunion, and my Uncle N. A. Fleming looked down at the big knot on my arm and said, "When did you break your arm?" Well, that made it official. Daddy took me to the doctor the next day, and the doctor had to rebreak and set my arm. I wore a heavy plaster cast for seven weeks, but that didn't stop me from riding Lindy.

Lindy had a bad habit about pulling back and breaking her bridle reins if we went off and left her tied. Daddy said we needed to be tying her with something heavier than those light leather reins. Daddy had grown up handling horses and mules, and he liked to tell us stories about a pair of old mules he used to farm with named "Kitty Kate" and "Red."

One day, Daddy decided he would like to plow the new garden with Lindy so he told me to go catch and harness the horse. Well, I had never harnessed a horse before, but I put everything on Lindy like I thought it should go and led her down to the garden. Daddy checked over the blind bridle, collar pad, collar, hames, and trace chains and said, "You've done pretty good, but you have the collar on up-side down." He soon got the collar turned around (the buckle is supposed to be on the top of the neck, not under like I had it) and started plowing. Lindy tolerated the plow-ing, but she must have thought this harness work was be-neath the dignity of such a fine riding horse because when Daddy stopped for lunch and tied her with a rope out by the garden, she promptly broke the rope and ran off to the barn. Daddy was not pleased. He got her back, finished plowing, and looped a trace chain around her neck and tied it to stout post oak tree. When he came back later, Lindy was lying on her back with all four feet in the air. Her head was about three feet off the ground and still firmly tied to the tree. I thought she was dead, but when Daddy got her loose, she got up and never again attempted to break a tie rope.

Greenville High School had what they called "Western Day" where all the high school seniors got to wear cowboy and cowgirl outfits and ride their horses to school. For a good part of my senior year, I had been planning for Western Day. I had bought a new gray felt cowboy hat, and Mom hired the lady down the road to make me a yellow satin western shirt with black stitching. I had been trying to train Lindy to load up in the stock trailer. However, Lindy wasn't having any part of that, and it looked like I might not have a horse to ride on Western Day. We lived nearly eight miles from the school building, and I didn't think I would have time to ride Lindy that distance and still make it to school on time. So after some more planning, I rode Lindy to Ardis Heights the evening before, left her at my friend Jerry Mainord's house overnight, and planned to ride her the rest of the way to school the next morning. All the way up to Ardis Heights that first evening, Lindy acted like she was so tired she couldn't take another step, but every time a truck passed, she tried to jump sideways. I also found out pretty quick Lindy didn't like to cross bridges (her hoofs made a hollow sound that spooked her). I was dreading crossing the long Highway 67 bridge over the Sabine River east of Greenville.

The next morning, Lindy and I left Jerry's house and headed toward Greenville. When we got to the Sabine River bridge, I waited until there wasn't a car in sight before we started across. We had made it about half way across the long bridge, and Lindy had her head up and was showing the whites of her eyes like she was about to bolt when I glanced behind and saw a vehicle way back but coming up fast. I tried to hurry Lindy along without giving her too much rein, and she was rolling her eyes and flicking her ears back and forth when the vehicle started blowing its horn a hundred yards back. The vehicle continued to blow its horn as it closed on me, and I was expecting the worst. We finally got off the bridge about the time a car pulled up beside me, and I saw it was my classmate Ronnie Money

Ronnie and Lindy Horse ready for Greenville Senior High School "Western Day," 1961. —Photo by Dorris George

who was just trying to be cute. Money had grown up on a farm himself and knew better than to honk a horn at a horse on a bridge. I was so mad I could have killed him, but mostly I was just glad to be alive.

Lindy and I made it the rest of the way to school OK. We had a good Western Day, and a lot of my classmates got to ride Lindy. Some who didn't have a horse even skipped class to keep on riding. I figured Lindy would be worn out when the day was done, but as soon as I crawled up on her and turned her head toward home, she broke into a trot. On the way home, she acted like an old hand around trucks and bridges. It had been an interesting day.

We had a whole series of unremarkable dogs at the farm, until we got a black and white border collie named "Rover." Someone was giving away free pups at the Market Square in Greenville, and Daddy brought one home. Rover was a cute little puppy who rapidly grew into the smartest dog I had ever seen. Border collies were supposed to be great livestock dogs, and Daddy said he had always wanted a dog that would help him herd cattle. Rover, however, never showed any interest in cows. Rover was a hunt'n' dog. He loved to chase rabbits, squirrels, and armadillos!

The "chase" of another kind was also important to Rover. He was the dominant male dog for about two miles in any direction, and he would disappear for a day or so at a time when there was a willing female to chase. These excursions away from home were sometimes hazardous to Rover's health.

On one still afternoon, I heard a shotgun blast and a dog yelp up to the north in the direction of the hog farm which was across Interstate 30 nearly a mile from the house. I recall thinking at the time, "That sounded like Rover," but then I dismissed it as unlikely; Rover had been around the house just a few minutes before. However, in about thirty minutes, Rover came limping home. His white fur was covered in blood. He just laid down under an oak tree in the backyard and didn't move. In those days, people generally didn't take a farm dog to the vet. So I got out the livestock penicillin and the big syringe with the needle that was about a millimeter in diameter and gave Rover a shot in the thigh. He didn't move. He still had not moved by the next day so I gave him another shot. On the third day, however, when I went to give him his shot, he wouldn't let me, and I knew he was going to get well.

The Mighty Rover Dog in action

—Photo by author

A year or so later, I heard the screech of vehicle brakes up on the Interstate followed by a "thud" and a "yelp!" Sure enough, it was Rover again. He came limping home covered in blood and laid down under his oak tree. We went through the same routine again, a shot of penicillin each day until he wouldn't let me give him a shot on the third day. You would think he would learn, but sometime later Rover was off visiting again and got himself torn up pretty bad in a fight with a pack of rival dogs. Same routine as before: Rover comes limping home covered in blood; Rover gets penicillin shots for two days; Rover refuses shot on third day; Rover is as good as new. That penicillin was wonderful stuff!

Although Rover stayed a little closer to home after that last episode, he apparently still thought of himself as Lord of the Manor. He would lie out in the front yard with his forepaws crossed, his head up, and his ears erect as he regally watched the world go by. I once happened to glance out in the front yard just in time to see Rover do a double take. His head jerked around and then jerked again like he could not believe what he was seeing. Rover rose smoothly and silently to his feet, all the time intently watching something in the distance. I moved around to the corner of the house and saw that Rover had seen a stray dog about a quarter of a mile away which had had the nerve to enter his territory.

Rover began to move toward his rival in an intense, cat-like stalk which became an excited, stiff-legged trot as he moved faster and faster toward the unsuspecting cur. Old Rover shifted gears about four times in that quarter mile, and by the time he got to the other dog, he was going flat out. The other dog never even saw what hit him. Rover threw his shoulder into that dog and rolled him a good fifteen feet. Rover didn't even bother to watch his victim quit rolling; he just threw his nose in the air, turned, and walked majestically back to the house. It was great to see the Mighty Rover Dog in action!

I really enjoyed farm animals, and all through my junior high and high school years, I thought I would grow up to be a cattle rancher. I took three years of vocational agriculture classes in high school, and was secretary-treasurer of the Greenville High School Chapter of the Future Farmers of America. By the time I got to college, however, my life had taken a different course.

Farm Work

"Rise and shine.
It's an old sun with a new splendor!"
—Daddy's wake-up call at the farm

My daddy loved hard work. When he was home from the railroad, he would always wake us up before daylight with his all-too-cheerful, "Rise and shine. It's an old sun with a new splendor!" When he was gone on an overnight railroad trip, he would leave us plenty of chores. Just as soon as he got back home, instead of resting like I thought he should, he would immediately find us some more work. We milked cows, vaccinated calves, cut firewood, built fences, dug ditches, plowed fields, shredded pastures, hauled hay, planted gardens, picked vegetables, and robbed bees.

It seemed like we were always working, but we seldom did anything the easy way, at least while Daddy was around. Daddy said he did things "by man strength and awkwardness." I suspect his particular style of farm work could have been the result of not having the money to hire additional help or buy farm machinery which would have made the work easier, but it may have just been something he learned from his daddy.

One day, Daddy and I were trying to repair the old rusty barbed wire fence south of the pear tree. We were tying the broken pieces of wire back together, and there didn't seem to be a strand of barbed wire more than ten feet long. I said, "Daddy, why don't we just buy some new wire." He kinda smiled and said, "I asked my daddy the same thing about this same fence a long time ago."

We burned a lot of wood in the fireplace. When we cut wood, Daddy would cut down tall, pole-sized post oak trees and trim off the limbs with his axe, Larry and I would saw up the poles into thirty-inch logs with our Sears bow saws, and Mike would pile brush. I remember once after we had already cut more firewood than we could possibly use for the rest of the winter, we had a unusual six-inch snow. We had already taken care of the farm animals and the whole family was in the house enjoying the fireplace when Daddy took us all down to the woods to cut some more firewood. I recall standing out in the cold with my feet freezing in thin rubber boots, sawing wood, and wondering why this chore couldn't have waited for a warmer day. I guess Daddy just felt like we ought to be working.

During the summer, Daddy had us clear trees for more garden space the hard way; we dug the trees up. I recall digging for days around the bases of several large blackjack oak trees. We slowly exposed and chopped off the feeder roots until we could finally cut the taproot. The tree would fall over taking its stump with it, and we would cut the tree up for firewood.

Daddy really seemed to enjoy digging water wells by hand and often reserved that particular chore for himself. He would first hire an old man at Campbell who was a "water witch" to come out and select the well site. The water witch would hold the forks of a Y-shaped green peach tree limb in each hand with the base of the Y pointed up. The old man would walk slowly along until the base of the peach tree limb pulled sharply downward toward water. He would then turn around, walk back the direction he had come from, count his steps until the limb quit pulling, and announce the depth of the water sand.

Once the well site was selected, Daddy would erect a tripod of three steel pipes or strong wooden poles over the site and attach a heavy chain and pulley at the top of the tripod. Daddy had a little hand-made posthole digger-looking thing about four inches in diameter and about five feet long. Daddy would jab the thing in the ground like you would to make a posthole, adding water as necessary to soften the ground. He then punched the mud out of the cylinder-shaped digger head with a stick. Once the hole was about four feet deep, Daddy would attach a one-inch diameter rope to an eye at the top of the digger and begin raising and dropping the heavy digger in the hole over and over again using the pulley for leverage. Each time the digger filled up with mud, Daddy would have to pull it all the way to the surface to punch out the mud.

Eventually, Daddy would hit a hard layer of shale or gravel, and he would have to pull his digger out of the hole and replace it with a thirty-five-pound steel cultivator axle, sharpened on one end like a rock bar. Once he had bounced the rock bar off the bottom of the hole a few times and pulverized some of the hard stuff, he would go back to using the digger to clean out the hole. This activity usually went on for days as the hole went slowly downward, eventually reaching water sand anywhere from fifty to a hundred feet below the surface. Daddy then replaced his digger with a specially-made, galvanized bucket that was the same diameter as the digger and about three feet long. The bucket had a flap in the bottom which opened when it hit the water and closed as it was raised back up the hole. Due to all the disturbance, the water was very muddy at first, but a few more bailings resulted in water which was only sorta muddy.

Daddy would then pour this water into a glass fruit jar and let it settle overnight. The next day, there would be a thin layer of mud at the bottom of the jar and clear water on top. Now was the moment of truth, time for the first taste! Sometimes it was pretty good, but sometimes it tasted strongly of iron and sulfur.

As I recall, Daddy dug at least three wells like that at the farm, but he never put a casing in any of them or used the wells in any way. He just wanted to know where the good water was in case he needed another water well.

Several years before, I had seen Daddy punch a fifty-foot deep test well at Daa's place in Campbell. Daddy found water he liked and set out to enlarge the test hole so he could insert a six-inch steel pipe casing to keep the hole from caving in on the sides. First, he used an eight-inch diameter posthole auger (the kind you use by twisting the wooden handles at the top around in a circle). It is hard work just to dig a three-foot deep posthole with this kind of

Daddy's wheelbarrow and augers he used to dig fifty-foot deep water wells.   —Photo by author

tool, but Daddy just kept adding more sections of pipe to the handle and then removing sections of pipe as he brought up each auger full of dirt. He would tie the auger pipe to an A-frame mounted above the hole as he was adding or removing pipe so the auger wouldn't fall to the bottom of the hole once the handles were removed. He worked at that hole for days, but eventually he had enlarged it all the way down to the water sand at fifty feet. At that point, Daddy decided the hole still wasn't big enough around, so he bought a used twelve-inch diameter auger from Texas Power and Light Company (the kind they once used to dig holes for utility poles before they had power augers). Work was even slower with the bigger auger, but Daddy kept at it, and he eventually completed the widening of the hole. However, when Daddy tried to get someone to install the casing pipe, they took one look at the hole and said it was just too crooked to get a casing down. Poor Daddy, at that point he had to hire a man with a machine to come in and drill a new well hole right beside the old one.

One of the most tedious jobs Daddy ever thought up for us to do involved fertilizing the Bermuda grass field. In the late 1950s, everyone was planting Coastal Bermuda for "improved pasture," and Daddy decided to plant the thirty-acre Big Field west of the house in this new wonder grass. Coastal Bermuda was a sterile hybrid which did not reproduce from seed; it could only be established by planting the roots or "sprigs." We spent nearly three weeks plowing, disking, and harrowing a seedbed over the entire thirty acres with our little two-row Ford tractor. Daddy then hired a man with a sprigging machine to plant the sprigs. The sprigging went OK, but then we didn't get any rain for more than two months.

Once it finally rained, most of the sprigs had dried up and died, and live Bermuda grass plants could only be seen every ten feet or so across the Big Field; the rest of the seedbed was mostly bare ground. Daddy wanted to save those surviving plants, but he felt like fertilizing the whole field with a tractor-drawn fertilizer spreader would be a waste of money because he would be fertilizing a lot of weeds between the scattered Bermuda grass plants. Daddy's solution was to get three galvanized steel buckets, fill them with granular commercial fertilizer, hand a bucket and a teaspoon to each of his boys, and tell us to go out and put a spoonful of fertilizer on each plant. It took us more than a week to cover the thirty acres, a spoonful at a time, but it worked. In only a few months, we had a solid stand of Coastal Bermuda that still produces hay today, more than fifty years later.

One type of farm work I didn't mind was robbing bees. For one thing, it didn't happen very often. We only had a couple of hives, just enough for our own use. Robbing bees was also quite an adventure. We put on long-sleeved shirts, tightly tied our shirt and trouser cuffs, put on our cheese cloth bee veils and leather gloves, lit up the bee smoker, and opened the top of the hive. Sometimes the bees were very docile, and we simply lifted frame after frame of beautifully-capped golden honey comb out of the hive, shook off the bees, cut the comb out of the wooden frames onto a large metal cookie sheet, and took it into the house.

At other times, particularly in damp weather, the bees would go crazy, and we had a fight on our hands. Bees would be hitting our veils, stinging our leather gloves, and buzzing like something out of a horror movie. I remember once when a bad swarm of bees followed Daddy all the way back to the house.

A couple of times, we even went out into the woods and cut wild bee trees and put those bees into new hives. We located bee trees by finding some flowers where a lot of bees were feeding. We then caught several bees in a glass fruit jar and released the bees one at a time as we followed them

George boys robbing bees at the farm, 1957. Note bee smoker used to pacify the bees prior to opening the hive.

—Photo by Cecil George

back to their bee tree. Once we had cut the bee tree down and split it open, we removed any good honey, located the queen, and put her in a new wooden hive we had brought along. If we couldn't find the queen, we put some of the old comb in the new hive, closed the lid, set the new hive on the ground close to the old bee tree and gently tapped on top of the new hive with a wooden stick over and over. I don't know why tapping on the bee hive worked, but the bees slowly crawled over and entered the new hive. After several days, we went down at night, blocked the hive's exit hole so the bees couldn't get out, and carried the new hive back to the house. Some of those wild bees, as well as some of the tame ones, were pretty feisty. We just think "killer bees" are something new. I read years later that blue-colored objects often anger bees. As I recall, most of our long-sleeved work shirts were light blue in color.

Farm Food

*"If you'll get me some eggs from the barn,
I'll make some boiled custard for Christmas."*
—My mom, Dorris Ridley George, c. 1958

One nice thing about living on the farm was the food. We had an orchard with peach trees, plum trees, pear trees, and grape vines. We also had a watermelon patch and a huge garden which produced sweet corn, tomatoes, okra, onions, potatoes, cantaloupes, several kinds of squash, and black-eyed, purple-hulled, cream, and brown crowder peas. Brown crowder peas cooked with salt pork and small, whole pods of okra were one of my favorites. We ate as much of the food as we could fresh, and Mom canned, froze, or gave away the rest.

We raised cattle and chickens for meat, milk, and eggs, and we used lots of milk and eggs prepared lots of ways including a thick Christmas drink we called "boiled custard." Mom said the recipe for boiled custard had been brought by her Hale family ancestors from Virginia to Texas in a covered wagon in 1849. The recipe called for cooking the milk, sugar, and other ingredients until it thickened, folding in beaten egg whites while the custard was still hot, and then flavoring the mixture with vanilla or lemon extract. Boiled custard was good served hot or cold.

The Jersey cows we had produced more cream than we could use, and a cup of hot chocolate served with a huge spoonful of raw cream was a fine drink on a cold day. Fresh black berries picked out in the pasture in late spring, served with mountains of fresh whipped cream, were also hard to beat. Mom churned butter, and we sometimes sold surplus cream at the Greenville Produce Market.

Occasionally, we had a spell of really cold weather, and all of the farm ponds froze over. When this happened, the cows couldn't drink, so we took an axe and chopped a hole in the ice. Sometimes, we gathered up the ice chips in a bucket, carried them back to the house, and made hand-cranked freezer ice cream in the garage. A big bowl of home-

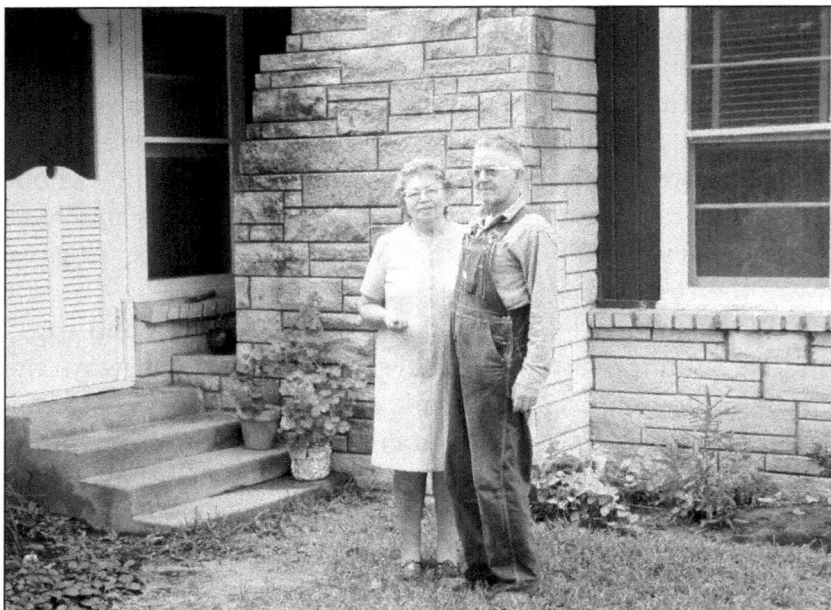

Cecil and Dorris George at the Farm on Timber Creek, 1973.
—Photo by author

made cherry ice cream went pretty well with a roaring fire in the fireplace.

Mom was a really great cook, and she usually had more than a dozen different dishes including maybe three kinds of potatoes on the table at every meal. She made really good fried chicken, veal loaf, and smothered steak. I often liked simple meals as well. Paw Paw Ridley and I really enjoyed a bowl of fresh cornbread with sweet milk (so named to distinguish it from buttermilk, I suppose). Daddy often told of having only a cold baked sweet potato to eat for his lunch many days when he was a school boy. The amazing thing was that he still enjoyed eating cold baked sweet potatoes for lunch the rest of his life.

On the days we were going to rob bees, Mom got up early and started baking huge pans of yeast rolls. By the time we came in the house with the honey, Mom would have hot rolls, homemade butter, and huge pitchers of fresh cold milk on the table. Farm food was good!

Farm Fun

"Don't you boys be trying to cross the creek."
—My mom, Dorris Ridley George, c. 1957

After we moved to the farm, Larry and I went swimming nearly every day during the summer in one of our farm ponds or in Mr. Spencer Hale's sandpit which was about a mile east of our house. Most of the farm ponds we swam in had clay bottoms and muddy water, but the sandpit with its sandy bottom had nice clear blue water. It was one of our favorite swimming holes.

One day, Larry and I caught some guys we didn't know swimming in the sandpit. Well, we sneaked around to where they had left their clothes, and I grabbed a pair of blue jeans to hide. However, as I picked up the jeans, I could tell from the weight that the guy had left his billfold, watch, and change in the pockets of the jeans. I didn't want to be accused of stealing someone's valuables, so I ran up on a high bare dirt bank about a hundred yards away and left the jeans spread out in plain sight. I guess he found them; the jeans were gone the next day.

Just for a change of pace, we would sometimes swim in a hole of standing water in Timber Creek on our farm. The Swimin' Hole on Timber Creek never dried up, even in the

66

drought of the '50s. It was shaded by big trees, and the water was always cool. The only problem with the Swimin' Hole was snakes. On several occasions, I recall seeing cottonmouths slide off the bank into the Swimin' Hole as we approached. Someone had told us cottonmouths couldn't bite under water so we went right in with them. We found out later, cottonmouths have no problem biting under water, but somehow we managed to survive those communal swims with the snakes.

One day, Larry and I discovered we could use a one-foot deep, four-foot by four-foot sheet-metal horse watering trough for a boat. It was a little cramped, but we could sit down in it and paddle around the Little Pool using wooden boards for oars. We eventually moved it to the Big Pool and ultimately to Timber Creek.

During much of the year, Timber Creek was just a twenty-foot wide, twelve-foot deep dry creek bed with a few holes of standing water. However, Timber Creek drained a sizeable watershed, and for several days after a major rain, it would flow lots of water. On one occasion, I recall we had had a big rain, and Timber Creek was way out of its banks. We could see from the house that the flood waters extended more than a hundred yards out into Mr. Pitt's pasture in some places. When we got in from school that afternoon, we changed clothes and started down to the creek. Before we got out of sight, Mom called us back and told us to not try to cross the creek. We said, "Yes, Ma'am" and headed off for our boat. We were planning to go down the creek, not across it.

Well, Larry and I got in our horse-trough boat and pushed off down The Mighty Timber Creek. We made the first eighty yards or so just fine. Then we came to a huge pile of fallen trees and driftwood which completely blocked the surface of the main channel. We tried to paddle over to one side, but the force of the water pinned our boat against the brush pile out in the middle of the creek. We found we couldn't move left or right, and when we tried to step out on the brushpile, it wouldn't support our weight. We were in a fix! The water was trying to come over the back of our boat and was gushing down through openings in the brush pile and threatening to take us with it. I am not sure how we finally got out of that mess, but we had had enough trouble for one day.

Hunting

"That is the biggest squirrel I've ever seen!"
—My Uncle Raymond George, c. 1960

When I was a small boy and we were still living in Commerce, Daddy would take Larry and me down to our farm near Greenville. Sometimes, Daddy would take along his Winchester .22-cal. bolt-action rifle. I think the rifle was a birthday or Christmas gift from Mom to Daddy right after they first married. Daddy kept the rifle broken down in its original box. When we got to the farm, Daddy would take the box out of the car and carefully fit the shiny-black, lightly-oiled barrel to the varnished walnut stock. As I recall, there was a screw in the forearm of the stock that held the barrel in place. The screw was designed to be tightened with a coin. The next step was to slip the bolt in place and lock it down. All the time Daddy was putting the rifle together he was explaining to us that a rifle was not a toy, and we had to be very careful around guns. Daddy then held the gun barrel up and let Larry and me take the bullets out of the box and carefully drop them, one at a time, through the bullet-shaped slot in the tubular magazine under the barrel. The bullets kept sliding down out of sight until the magazine was finally full.

We had already set up some tin cans for targets on a board by the old house place, and Daddy checked one last time to make sure we were standing behind him with our hands over our ears. Then Daddy took careful aim. There was a loud, ringing "POW," and a can jumped off the board! At the time, I didn't think there could be any rifle more powerful than that .22. After Daddy fired several times, he would carefully hold the rifle and let first Larry, and then me, look down the sights and pull the trigger. We didn't hit many cans, but this was a big-time adventure! I will never forget picking up spent .22 hulls, sniffing the acrid, sweet odor of burned gun powder, marveling at the technology, and wondering if I would ever be able to shoot a gun like that by myself. When we finished shooting, Daddy would carefully clean, disassemble, and place the rifle back in its box until our next trip.

I was still too young to follow Daddy around the farm on a real hunting trip, but Larry got to go along sometimes. I was about six years old when I finally saw Daddy shoot a cottontail rabbit with the .22. He killed it stone-cold dead with one shot from about eighty feet away. The rabbit was sitting about where we planted the magnolia tree in the front yard of the new farm house several years later. I recall that hunt as clearly as if it happened yesterday. My brother Mike still has that old rifle.

Daddy was concerned about the danger of a .22 bullet carrying a long way and injuring someone. The ammunition box said, "Danger! range one mile." So even after we moved to the farm in 1955, Larry and I didn't get to go hunting with Daddy's rifle for a long time. What we used was BB guns.

Larry and I got quite good with our BB guns in shooting cans, grasshoppers, cotton rats, and anything else which offered a good target. I remember walking around the Big Pool many times trying to pop water snakes, leopard frogs, and bullfrogs with my BB gun. As I recall, most of the frogs jumped into the water and got away, but when they came up out in the middle of the pool, we would get down low and try to skip BBs across the water toward the frog. My best record was three BB skips on top of the water before it hit a bullfrog. I eventually carved five notches in the wooden stock of my Daisy "Red Ryder" lever-action BB gun to record the five cottontail rabbits I bagged with that gun.

My brother Mike came in one fall day to show us a mourning dove he had bagged with his BB gun. He claimed he had shot it out of the air. Of course, we figured he was making that up. A few days later, he came in with another dove and the same story. Again, he was ridiculed by his older brothers. A few days later, however, Mike and I were walking back to the house across Mr. Pitt's pasture when a dove happened to fly over us. Mike dropped to the ground on his right knee, put the stock of his BB gun against the top of his right leg just above the knee, pointed the barrel skyward in the general direction of the dove, and rapidly pulled the trigger and pumped his BB gun three times, "Pop, Pop, Pop" like an anti-aircraft gun. On the third pop, the dove tumbled out of the air, shot through the head! Heck, he wasn't even looking down the barrel! I still don't know how he did it.

For Christmas one year, Santa Claus brought us a J. C. Higgins, 20-gauge single-shot, break-action shotgun. Suddenly, nothing in Hunt County was safe from the George boys. I bagged my first swamp rabbit and my first jack rabbit with that shotgun. Eventually, I even got to where I could stalk crows harassing an owl and get close enough to shoot one of those ever-wary crows out of the air.

The most impressive thing I ever bagged with the 20-gauge was a gray fox. It had been raining heavily, and I was walking around in the creek bottom wearing rubber boots. All of a sudden, I saw a movement to my left and realized a gray fox had run up toward me on the other side of a little brush-lined slough and stopped about fifteen feet away. I instinctively shouldered the gun and fired. It was a beautiful animal. I skinned it out and stretched and salted the hide. When it was good and dried, I asked Mom if I could hang the hide on the wall in the den. We had knotty pine paneling in the den, and I thought the old fox would look pretty good on that paneling. I was absolutely amazed when she agreed. I recall the first time Uncle Raymond came in the house after I had hung up the fox hide. He took one look at it and said, "That is the biggest squirrel I've ever seen!" I was insulted! Larry still has that old 20-gauge.

A few years later, Uncle Clifford loaned us his Winchester Model 12, pump-action, 12-gauge shotgun for us to use in "hunting wolves." The wolves, which were really coyotes, were showing up regularly on the farm after being run out of the Sabine River bottomlands further downstream by the construction and flooding of Lake Tawakoni. We never did shoot any wolves with the gun, but I sure shot a hole through the dining room ceiling with it. It was really cold that day, and I had been out hunting with the Model 12. I knew better than to come in the house with a loaded gun. I had never done that before in my life. However, my fingers felt so cold I didn't think I could work the pump release button in front of the trigger guard. I recall thinking I could do that much better after I warmed my hands up by the fireplace. Well, anyway, I walked in the house and backed up to the roaring fireplace in the den. After I had warmed up a few minutes, I was sorta cradling the shotgun in my arms with the barrel pointed in the general direction of the dining room when I started trying to find the pump release button. The next thing I knew, there was a horrible roar, and plaster dust was raining down out of the ceiling over the dining room table! I expected Mom to be yelling at me. After all, she was cooking dinner at the stove about six feet from the hole in the ceiling, but there wasn't a sound around the corner in the kitchen. I was afraid I had somehow hit her! I cautiously said, "Mom, are you all right?" She said she was. She said she was just holding her breath thinking I had killed everybody in the den.

George boys with Freddy Bennett (white shirt) and Rover Dog fix'n to go hunt'n at the farm, c. 1963. —Photo by Dorris George

Well, Larry, Mike, and I got real busy plastering up the hole in the ceiling before Daddy got home. I thought he would be really mad, but he just told me to be more careful. He knew how bad I felt about bringing a loaded gun in the house. Years later, Uncle Clifford gave me the Model 12 to keep. I have it still.

It was a special treat when Uncle Clifford and Uncle Raymond and his sons (our cousins) Joe and Ray George came to the farm to hunt squirrels and rabbits. It was one of the few times Daddy would let us take the whole day off. He would sometimes go along with us. These hunts often took all Saturday morning and part of Saturday afternoon. Mom always had a big dinner ready for us when we got home. We learned a lot in those days about family and friends, wildlife, hunter safety, and fair chase.

Many years later, Larry was hunting mule deer in the Snake River Breaks in Washington when he saw a coyote caught in a government trapper's steel leghold trap. As Larry walked down to take a closer look, he saw the ground was all torn up around the trap, and the coyote was caught by one front paw. The coyote looked exhausted and didn't struggle but simply lay there watching him intently. Larry got to feeling sorry for the poor old coyote waiting in the trap for its fate. Messing with any wild animal, particularly one that feels threatened, is a good way to get hurt, but Larry started talking quietly to the coyote and slowly approached the trapped animal. The coyote's intense yellow eyes never wavered from his. Larry unslung his old Springfield 30-06 rifle and held it low as he took one step at a time closer to the coyote. Eventually, he got close enough to step on the trap chain and hold it down. As Larry slowly slid his feet, an inch at a time, up the trap chain, the coyote continued to watch. Holding his rifle between him and the coyote, Larry eventually got to where he could place his right hunting boot on one spring of the double-spring trap. With the yellow eyes still locked on his, Larry eased his rifle around and placed the stock of his rifle on the other spring. As Larry pressed down on the springs, the trap jaws fell open, and the coyote slowly withdrew its paw from the trap. The coyote continued to lie where it was, intently watching Larry as he turned to walk away. When Larry glanced back, the coyote was gone. Larry said it was one of the best hunts he had ever been on.

Fishing

*"Mommie, Mommie, we killed
a poppa head snake!"*
—Me, c. 1947

I must have been about four years old when Daddy took Larry and me on my first fishing trip. We dug up some earthworms for bait in the backyard of our home in Commerce, tied two long cane fishing poles to the top of our old Model A Ford, and drove south of Commerce on the Campbell Road to the Sulfur River. We crossed the rickety boards on the old steel trestle bridge and parked on the south side of the river. We got out, gathered up our poles and other gear, and started walking east through the river-bottom timber. We hadn't gone far when Daddy suddenly stopped us and whispered, "There's a poppa head snake!" Daddy told us it was poisonous and for us to be real still. Daddy eased around, picked up a handy stick, and whacked the snake a good one. I was certainly impressed!

After Daddy dispatched the snake, we moved on down to the riverbank, and Daddy rigged up our cane poles with braided fishing line, cork bobbers, small lead weights that clamped to the line, and fishhooks. The next step involved threading a wriggling worm onto the hook and swinging the line out into the water. The cork bobbers floated quietly on the surface. Daddy stuck the end of each pole into the mud and climbed back up the steep muddy riverbank.

We had only waited a few minutes when one of the cork bobbers twitched! After a few seconds, the bobber twitched again and then jerked under the muddy water. Just as Daddy got down the slippery bank to the pole, the cork came up again and began to move slowly around on the surface. Daddy got the pole out of the mud and just held it quietly. All of a sudden, the cork disappeared under water again, and Daddy hauled back on the pole bending it into an arc. Out of the water and up into the air flew a wildly thrashing fish. Once Daddy got the fish safely up on the bank, he showed it to Larry and me and said it was a catfish. It had a bunch of worm-like whiskers around its mouth, and the whole fish might have been eight inches long. It certainly looked like we were having a successful fishing trip! Daddy caught one more smaller catfish, and we gathered up our gear and called it a day. As soon as we got back home, I went running into the house telling Mom about the "poppa head snake." Later, Daddy explained to me it was really a "copperhead" snake. Daddy cleaned the catfish in the kitchen sink, and Mom rolled them in corn meal and fried them in hot bacon grease. They tasted delicious!

Several years later while we were building the new house at the farm, I recall catching grasshoppers for fish bait and fishing at the Little Pool with a chinaberry limb and one of those new red and white plastic bobbers. Right at sunset one evening, I caught a rockbass which was the biggest fish I had ever seen anyone catch. It might have weighed three quarters of a pound.

We fished a lot in the Big Pool at the farm and often set out trotlines with multiple hooks or left cane poles stuck in the bank. Mostly, we caught small sunfish we called "perch" and bullhead catfish we called "catfish."

I recall leaving a switch cane pole set out one night, and when I came back the next morning, the pole was gone! After a short search, we saw the pole floating out in the middle of the pool. Every once in a while as we watched, we could see the pole tremble a little and move slowly to another spot. Something would have to be done about this! We kept a pair of old swim trunks back in the brush for just such an emergency, and I quickly changed into them and slipped out into the water. I got ahold of the pole, towed it to the bank, and slowly began to pull in the line. Nothing happened at first. Then there was a big splash, and I got my first glimpse of the biggest yellow bullhead catfish I had

George boys on a fishing trip in Arkansas, early 1950s.
—Photo by Dorris George

ever seen. We got the fish safely out of the water and up on the bank. It was a really nice fish! We didn't have any way to weigh it, but we took it up to the garage and used Daddy's carpenter's square to measure it. As I recall, it was exactly fifteen and a half inches long. After we showed the fish off some more, Mom cooked it for supper. About thirty years later, I was looking through the official list of "State Record Fish" certified by the Texas Parks and Wildlife Department when I saw someone had just caught a yellow bullhead which had been certified as the new state record for the species. Their fish was only fourteen inches long. We had eaten the Texas State Record Yellow Bullhead thirty years before without even knowing it!

Arrowheads

*"These arrowheads were made
by Indians a long time ago."*
—My daddy, Cecil George, c. 1948

When I was a small boy growing up in Commerce, I recall Daddy showing us a child's shoebox containing a dozen or more delicate flint Indian arrowheads he had found around the farm over the years. Even more impressive than the arrowheads, however, was a perfect tomahawk head chipped from white flint. Daddy let us carefully handle the fragile artifacts as he speculated about how they were made and about the people who made them long ago.

When we moved to the farm, I couldn't wait to start hunting arrowheads. Daddy said it was best to go out after a rain had washed everything clean. Right away, I found a lot of flint chips created in the manufacture of arrowheads and other artifacts, but it was a long time before I found my first arrowhead. It didn't look like much, but it was definitely an arrowhead made by an ancient hunter. Slowly, I got better and better at seeing arrowheads. Some nights, I would even dream about finding a particular color of arrowhead such as a red or white one, which were uncommon, and then I would go out the next day and find one just like

I had dreamed about. I eventually discovered from reading that many of the "arrowheads" we had been finding were really "dart points" made to be used on throwing spears propelled by an "atlatl," or throwing stick, thousands of years before the invention of the bow and arrow.

One of the most unusual artifacts I ever found was a smooth, dark brown tomahawk head which appeared to been made of clay and then fired like pottery. I found it in a sandpit near the farm. The tomahawk head was broken into a dozen or more pieces when I found it, but it fit back together like a jigsaw puzzle. My personal collection of about three hundred artifacts has now been photographed and recorded for posterity by the Texas State Archeologist, but that first misshapen arrowhead I found still has a place of honor in the center of the top row of my first frame of arrowheads.

As a high school student, I even thought about becoming an archeologist myself, but closer investigation revealed there were very few jobs at that time for professional archeologists. Besides, I was planning to be a chemist. In the early 1960s, I recall a chemical company promoting, "Better things for better living through chemistry." That seemed to be where the jobs were, and that was what I planned to major in when I went to college.

Pea Thrashers

"But Larry's pea thrashers always work!"
—My daddy, Cecil George, c. 1960

Daddy was a good rough carpenter who could build things with his hands. He always had a dream, however, of building something special like a perpetual motion machine that would continue to operate without using fuel or a pea thrasher that would really thrash peas. He figured perfecting and patenting either of these inventions would be personally satisfying and perhaps financially rewarding. Although Daddy could never make either of his inventions work, he did enjoy watching Larry's chemical, mechanical, and electronic experiments. He called them "Larry's Pea Thrashers."

Larry had a little workshop down in the garage where he kept his *Popular Mechanics* and *Popular Electronics* magazines, sent off mail-orders for scientific materials, conducted experiments, and built various gadgets. Some of the gadgets were quite complex, and Larry had to modify and improvise to get the results he wanted. During his junior year in high school, Larry built a Van de Graaff generator which gathered static electricity and transferred it by means of a motor-driven latex belt up to a six-inch steel sphere which had seen an earlier life as a model globe of the world. Once the machine had run a few seconds, the globe would give off a crackling electrical spark several inches long to any object held near it. If you put your hands on top of the globe and then started the generator, it would make your hair stand on end!

Larry's senior year science project was a Tesla coil, another electronic contraption, which was far more complicated than the Van de Graaff generator. Larry ordered some parts and built a special spool device to smoothly roll more than a hundred feet of very fine copper wire tightly around a two-foot tall Plexiglas cylinder. He then mounted the innards of the machine on a varnished mahogany board and enclosed it all in a Plexiglas box he had built. The Tesla coil was a beautiful piece of equipment just sitting there. When he turned it on, however, it was awesome!

The Tesla coil emitted a buzzing sound and shot continuous lavender-colored electronic "flames" out the top of the coil. If he held a newspaper in the flames, it would immediately set the paper on fire, but you could run your hand quickly through the flames without effect! If he held a neon or florescent light tube near the coil, the tube would light up just like it was plugged in. He could even "squeeze" the light down the tube with his hand! This was all very impressive to a bunch of high school students and apparently to science fair judges as well. Larry's Tesla coil took first place at the 1960 Greenville High School Science Fair!

Larry's next project was a digital computer which used a rotary telephone dial to input the data. I didn't begin to understand all of this, but the whole family was very proud of Larry. It was just as well Mom and Daddy didn't know about some of Larry's other experiments.

Larry made a handheld spotlight out of an old automobile headlight. On Sunday evenings after church, we would open the hood of Old Blue, our family's 1950 Chevrolet

Larry with one of his "pea thrashers" at the 1960 Greenville High School Science Fair. His Tesla coil sprouted lavender-colored electronic "flames" at the top and could light up unattached florescent bulbs held nearby.

—Photographer unknown

sedan, fasten the spotlight wires to the car battery under the hood, and drive around "Old Number 5," the big Greenville Water Works reservoir, spotlighting romantic couples parked in the darkness. It is a wonder we didn't get shot!

We were spotlighting airplanes around Major's Field one night when the entire world around us lit up as bright at day. We could see fences, buildings, and pastures several miles away. I was scared to death; I thought we had either been caught by airport security or the world was coming to an end. We seemed to be in serious trouble! I was sitting in the middle of the front seat and couldn't see out much, but Larry was driving and he leaned over to the left, looked out the side window, and saw a huge meteor disappearing to the north. We drove across Greenville to the broadcasting studio of Radio Station KGVL and listened to all of the reports coming into the station from concerned citizens who had "seen the light" but didn't know what it was.

Our Uncle N. A. Fleming gave Larry an eight-inch diameter electric bell which Larry promptly mounted under Old Blue. Whenever we were stopped in heavy traffic at a red light on Lee Street, Larry would turn on the bell, and we would look around like everyone else trying to figure where all the noise was coming from.

Larry also rigged up a radio speaker in the car's front grill and hooked it up to a microphone through the car's radio so he could talk to strangers walking down the sidewalk. You often couldn't tell where the voice was coming from, and we got some really puzzled looks from folks.

Shocking Tails

"Ronnie, you want a ride into town?"
—My brother Larry, c. 1959

Just when things seemed to be getting dull, Larry ordered the Model T spark coil from the Sears Automotive Supply Catalog. This contraption had been designed to provide the ignition in one of the first Ford automobiles, and it delivered a powerful electrical shock. I should have been suspicious when Larry kindly offered to drive me into town. As soon as I sat down in the front passenger's seat of Old Blue, Larry touched a button hidden under the seat, and the spark coil sent an electric current to a sheet of aluminum foil Larry had slid under the front seat cover. The shock really lifted me off the seat!

After I got over being mad, I couldn't wait to try it on Freddy Bennett, James Martin, and some of our other teenage friends. We quickly shocked all of our buddies, and it got to where nobody wanted to ride in the front seat. No sweat, Larry just put a new sheet of aluminum foil under the seat cover all the way across the back seat. He got three at a time with this new arrangement!

After a college football game at East Texas State one night, we offered a ride to a band member James Martin knew. We got up to about 5 MPH before Larry touched the control button. The band guy, in his spiffy new uniform, screamed and jumped out of the car! There was a terrible scraping noise in the road gravel, and the guy wouldn't get back in the car with us. Some people just don't have a sense of humor!

Larry's next project was to move some spark coil wires around and electrically charge the outside of the old Chevy. This arrangement required an electrical ground to complete the circuit. It was my job to hold a grounding chain up the outside of the passenger's door with a string, drop it when we got in position, and pour a cup of water on the chain to ensure a good ground.

Well, we loaded up Freddy and James and a bunch of the other guys and went to a drive-in restaurant on south Wesley Street in Greenville, where we knew an attractive carhop who always leaned on our car door when she was taking our order. As soon as we parked, I dropped the chain and poured the water while Larry got his control button ready. Right on schedule, the carhop pranced out to our car and bent over to take our order. When her left elbow was just about to touch the car door, Larry pushed his control button, and a crackling, blue-green spark about an inch long jumped to her elbow!

The carhop jumped back and said things that would have embarrassed a sailor. Larry began to apologize to the carhop and tell her about the bad electrical short we had in the car's wiring and that he had been trying to get it fixed. By now, the carhop had calmed down some, and she was buying Larry's line when one of our "friends," walked up from another car and said, "Did he get you with that old shocker trick?" That set off some more bad words from the carhop, and she left without taking our order. Sometimes it's just hard to get good service at a drive-in.

When Larry was a freshman in college, he ordered a

couple of six-foot diameter, military-surplus weather balloons. He then borrowed some hydrogen and oxygen cylinders from somewhere, and he and some of his college buddies went out one night to a sandpit south of Commerce that was sort of a lover's lane. Larry and his crew quickly filled a weather balloon about a third full of oxygen, added enough hydrogen until it floated, capped it off, and played the balloon out on a fifty-foot electrical wire tether. There was quite a wind that night which caused the balloon to bounce along the ground rather than floating majestically overhead. Larry got out his trusty Model T spark coil and sent a spark down the wire to the balloon. The world turned green, and the concussion nearly knocked them down! There had been a couple of guys target shooting on the back side of the sandpit, several dogs barking in the distance, crickets chirping, and other night noises before the blast, but after the blast, there was total silence!

Larry and his crew quickly stomped out a small grass fire the explosion had caused, loaded up their gear in two vehicles, and raced for the gate. Larry's car got through OK, but the farmer who owned the sandpit roared up in his pickup and blocked the second car. John Phelps, the driver of that car, was a quick thinker. He yelled to the farmer, "Back up, back up, they're getting away!" The farmer threw his pickup into reverse, and the second car roared off "in pursuit" of the first car! Various reports later attributed the explosion to bank robbers, hand grenades, dynamite, and maybe an alien landing. They never did suspect a pea thrasher!

Could Have Been Worse

"Stolen watermelons are sweeter."
—My father-in-law, Ed Hejl

There many times when we got into scrapes that could have turned out a lot worse than they did. For example, my brother Mike and his friend David Bearden had parked Old Blue on a sandy country road, climbed over a barbed wire fence, and were selecting a watermelon to swipe out of a neighbor's patch when they saw the neighbor's pickup truck coming up the road. They leaped over the fence and ran for the car. Unfortunately, Mike's bare foot landed on an upturned rusty garden rake that was hidden in the grass. Three of the tines pierced Mike's instep. His foot was bleeding badly, but he managed to hobble to the car. Bearden drove, and they made their getaway without being caught. Mike's foot was so badly injured he was afraid he wouldn't be able to play high school football that season, but after swabbing his puncture wounds with Campho-Penique (a standard 1950s East Texas miracle drug treatment for all injuries short of broken bones), Mike was nearly as good as new. Forty years later, he still has a line of scars across the bottom of his foot. It could have been worse.

About the first time Freddy Bennett came down to the

farm, Mike and I were showing him around when we came to Timber Creek. We had a place where we usually crossed the creek by swinging across on a severed possum grape vine that was hanging down from a tall wateroak tree. The grape vine was about an inch thick and plenty stout to support our weight, but you had to pick your feet up to clear the far bank. I demonstrated the creek-crossing technique to Freddy and handed him the vine. Freddy had apparently been talking and not listening (surprise, surprise) and missed the part about picking up his feet. Anyway, Freddy sung gracefully across the water with his hefty body extended full length and smacked heavily into the far bank with a resounding "WHOOMP." He looked like a sack of cement on the end of a rope. It was impressive to watch. Fortunately, Freddy didn't lose his grip on the vine and fall into water, but he was pretty shook up. It could have been worse.

My mom's Cousin Lucille gave Larry and me an old radio that really should have been given to a museum. It had a beautiful varnished wooden case about eighteen inches long and eight inches high with a sloped instrument panel in front. The instrument panel had an on/off switch, a volume control, and a tuning knob. You could lift the heavy, hinged lid and look inside at the parts. Larry was really interested in the rheostat that controlled the volume and the two wire coils that you could move to control radio frequency. Larry removed the parts so he could study them better. I had other plans for the case. Sure enough, after I slid the instrument panel out through the top, I could insert a clear pane of glass in its place, and I had a perfect snake cage. Along about that time, we noticed a newspaper advertisement from a place in El Paso that bought snakes. The advertisement said that if you would send them $10, the snake buyers would send you their price lists and procedures for shipping snakes. Well, we sent our check to the snake buyers but never heard back from them. It was apparently just a case of mail fraud to get our money. It could have been worse; we could have actually been sending snakes through the U.S. Mail.

Several years later, Mike found a copperhead at the farm and thought he should capture it. Mike penned the venomous snake down with a stick, caught it carefully behind the head with his fingers and thumb, and picked it up. To his horror, the snake slowly squirmed around in his hand, opened its mouth, and stuck one fang in the side of his thumb! Mike was so embarrassed about his poor snake handling, he didn't say anything to anyone about it until several months later. I guess it was a good thing the snake was unable to get any venom into the wound. It could have been worse.

I was driving cows to the barn when a summer thunderstorm caught me out in the open. Lightning was popping in the distance, but it wasn't very close, and I was avoiding walking under any trees. I got to one place, however, where I had to drive the cows down a lane between two rows of trees about a hundred feet apart (there just wasn't any other way to get to the barn and the rain was getting heavier by the minute). As I was about to get through the tight spot, a lightning bolt that appeared to be eight inches in diameter hit a dead elm tree fifty feet to my right. There was a tremendous crash! One second the tree was there and the next it was just a shower of flaming toothpicks falling to the ground. The cows and I hurried on toward the barn. It could have been worse.

The summer after I finished high school, Larry and I thought we should organize a hay ride for our Wesley Methodist Church youth group. We hitched our 1950 Ford tractor to a big four-wheel hay trailer we had borrowed somewhere and scattered some loose hay on the trailer. We met at Dennis Smith's house east of Greenville and loaded up a couple of adult counselors, several teenage couples, and a few singles. Larry was driving the tractor, and I was riding in back with my date. Larry was supposed to travel by the most direct route on the back roads to a roadside park on Interstate 30 where we were to meet the other counselors and have a wiener roast at about 9 P.M. Larry, however, took a longer route. I knew we were in trouble when I realized we were fix'n to top Pilot Knob, a high hill overlooking the Sulfur River bottoms between Greenville and Commerce. As he started down Thrill Hill, Larry thought he would just slip the tractor out of gear, get up some speed, and give everyone some excitement. As we bounced down the narrow dirt road with the tractor's weak headlamps barely illuminating the deep ditches on either side, it was quickly apparent to me that we were going way too fast! Larry tried to slow us down with the old, worn-out brakes that barely worked on level ground. The trailer started to fishtail back and forth! Larry, in desperation, jammed the gearshift lever back in gear. There was a terrible clashing of gears, but the tractor decelerated rapidly. This caused the slick hay, and all of the people on the trailer, to slide forward. There were no sideboards of any kind, and it is a wonder that someone didn't fall off the front edge of the trailer and go under the wheels. Larry eventually got us stopped and turned around. When we finally got to the picnic area, the other counselors were worried about us being so late. It could have been worse.

A couple of years after Larry and I left home, Mike was riding one Sunday evening after church with our cousin, Gary Fleming, in his dad's 1950 yellow Jeepster convertible. As they left Greenville, a big fuzzy dog charged out of the darkness from a farm house and began to bark furiously at the right front wheel of the car. Impulsively, Mike picked up a BB pistol (that they just happened to have on the front seat) and popped the dog on the rump with a BB. The dog quickly lost all interest in cars, but the dog's owner saw what Mike had done. The dog owner leaped off his porch and raced for his car. Gary floor-boarded the Jeepster and made for the back roads along the Sabine River. As Gary was racing along on the narrow dirt roads through the gathering darkness, he saw an open field gate and whipped in there to throw off his pursuer. Unfortunately, there was a water-filled slough just inside the gate, and there was a big "SPLASH!" Gary turned off his headlights, but they never saw the other car. After everything got quiet, Gary turned on his headlights, and they saw the Jeepster was standing in about three feet of water and mud. Mike got out of the car in his church clothes and began to push the vehicle while Gary gunned the engine. After about a half hour of this, they managed to get the Jeepster out of the slough. They drove to a coin-operated car wash and managed to wash most of the mud off themselves and the Jeepster. Mike's clothing had pretty well air-dried by the time they got back to the farm, and Mike managed to sneak into the house with being caught. It could have been worse.

Road Warriors

"Are you Melvin Morris?"
—Dallas Road Warrior, 1964

I learned to drive Old Blue, our family's 1950 Chevy, when I was in driver's education class in the ninth grade. Up until that time, Larry was the only one besides my folks who got to drive our car. After church on Sunday mornings when I was in driver's ed, I would usually be allowed to practice my driving on the half mile of country road leading from our house up to Interstate 30. It was easy to drive on the nearly level country road, but when I had to turn around on the steep slope leading up to the stop sign at the Interstate (there was no service road there in those days), I had trouble managing the brakes, clutch, stick shift, and accelerator all at once. Over time, however, I mastered it and sorta grew up with that vehicle. I took my driver's test, dated my first girls, and later commuted to college at East Texas State in Old Blue.

Jumping ahead several years to the summer of 1964, I had been visiting my girlfriend Barbara at her parent's home in Lancaster and was returning to Greenville along Interstate 30 east of Dallas about midnight in Old Blue. There was hardly any traffic on the road, but I noticed a

94

tan-colored 1952 Chevy sedan enter the highway from an entry ramp up ahead, and the vehicle sorta jerked once or twice like the driver might have been drinking. I was traveling about 65 MPH, which was about all Old Blue would do, when I passed the other car.

The driver of the other car let me get well past him and change back into the right lane before he sped up and pulled along the left side of me and began blowing his horn. I looked over and saw two men and a woman, all in their thirties, in the front seat of the vehicle. I didn't recognize any of them so I just kept driving on toward Greenville at the same speed.

After honking several more times, the other vehicle slowed down and gradually dropped back until its headlights disappeared far behind me. I didn't have any idea what that was all about, but I had a bad feeling about that vehicle. A couple of times I thought about exiting the Interstate and going on to Greenville along some back roads, but it was late and I was tired, and the Interstate was the most direct route back to Greenville.

I had driven several more miles when I saw the glow of headlights behind me again. The headlights came up fast, and sure enough, it was the same '52 Chevy. The other car pulled up on the left side of me again, and the driver began to honk his horn. The man on the passenger's side was waving his arm out his window for me to stop my car. I wasn't about to stop! This went on for several minutes, and we came up on two semi-trucks. I tried to get between the semis, hoping I would discourage the '52 Chevy but without any luck. After a while, we had passed the semis, and the honking and waving was still going on when the driver of the other car suddenly swerved over into my lane and forced me over onto the shoulder and then out into the grass along the right of way! It was all I could do to get Old Blue stopped without hitting the other car. I dropped my gear shift into low and was trying to get around the other vehicle and back on the pavement when the man on the passenger's side said with menace in his voice, "You better stop!"

I was so scared and he said it so forcefully, I stopped. The driver got out of his vehicle, stepped over to my car and said, "Are you Melvin Morris?" Well, I was never so glad in all my life I wasn't Melvin Morris! I said, "No," and he said, "Let me see your driver's license." I got my billfold out but couldn't get my license out of the little see-through holder so I just handed him my wallet which only had a couple of dollars in it. He took a look at my license, handed my billfold back, and said, "Sorry." He then got back in his vehicle, and they all drove off. I was so shook, I stalled my engine, and had trouble restarting it.

I never got their license plate number or anything, and I still don't know who Melvin Morris was or why they wanted him. They obviously didn't know him on sight. I can only conclude he drove a vehicle similar to Old Blue. From their behavior, I have often thought they might have been small-town cops who had had too much to drink. Whoever they were, if they ever caught up with Melvin Morris, he was going to be in trouble!

Air Force Blue

"They took the blue from the skies
and a pretty girl's eyes
and a touch of Old glory's hue,
And gave it to the men who proudly wear
the U.S. Air Force blue."
　　　　　—"U.S. Air Force Blue," Department of
　　　　　Defense newsreel song, 1957

Larry, Mike, and I all attended East Texas State University (ET) at Commerce, Texas, where we enrolled in the Air Force Reserve Officers Training Corps (AFROTC). By the time he graduated in 1964, Larry was a cadet colonel and the Commander of the Corps of Cadets. I was a cadet major and a squadron commander. Mike says he can't remember his cadet rank. We were all commissioned as second lieutenants in the U.S. Air Force upon graduation.

After graduation at ET, Larry deferred active military duty so he could attend graduate school at Washington State University at Pullman. Later, Larry served at bases throughout the United States in the Biomedical Sciences Corps specializing in laboratory medicine and computers. Larry retired from the Air Force as a lieutenant colonel in 1997 with twenty-eight years of service. Mike and I always

AFROTC cadets Ronnie and Larry George in dress uniforms with sabers, 1964.   —Howse Photography, Commerce, Texas

suspected Larry was really with the CIA; he hung around with some really strange people in Washington, D.C.

I entered pilot training at Webb Air Force Base at Big Spring, Texas, in April 1965 and received the silver wings of an Air Force pilot in May 1966. I attended KC-135 jet

USAF officers Ron, Mike, and Larry George in mess dress uniforms at Mike's wedding, 1972.   —Photo by Barbara George

tanker aircraft school at Castle AFB in California and later served in Texas, Alaska, Greenland, and Southeast Asia. My crew and I pulled alert duty in the "Mole Hole" and flew 28 combat air refueling mission during the Vietnam Conflict logging over two hundred hours of combat air time. We witnessed the Communist Tet Offensive in South Vietnam and the *Pueblo* Incident in Korea. When I left the Air Force in 1970 as a captain with a regular commission, I was

USAF 1/Lt. Ron George's KC-135 jet tanker aircraft refueling an F-100 jet fighter over Laos during Vietnam Conflict, 1968.   —Photo by author

thought to be the youngest aircraft commander in the Strategic Air Command since World War II.

Mike entered pilot training at Columbus AFB, Mississippi, in 1971. During his eight-year Air Force career, Mike first served as a "Hurricane Hunter" flying huge four-engine HC-130 aircraft into the eye of hurricanes to measure storm conditions for weather forecasting at Ramey AFB, Puerto Rico, and later at Keesler AFB, Mississippi. He later took on the only slightly less risky job of teaching Iranian exchange students to fly T-38 supersonic jet trainers. Mike left the Air Force as a captain in 1979 and became an airline pilot.

Photos of the George boys and their airplanes that hung on the wall at the George farmhouse for many years.

Weather Conjuring

*"The wind can't blow like this for three days
without it blowing up something."*
—My mother, Dorris Ridley George, c. 1950

Did I ever tell you about the time I conjured up weather and shut down flying during my Air Force pilot training days? Well, the story actually started much earlier when I was growing up on the family farm near Greenville in Northeast Texas.

Both Mom and Daddy were farm people who spent a lot of time outdoors and watched the weather as it affected their lives and livelihood. Mom had to know when a cloud was coming up so she could get the baby chicks or turkey poults inside, and Daddy, of course, liked to get his crops planted or the new hay in the barn before it started raining. Daddy in particular liked to sit in the cool of the evening and watch the sunset. Later, when he came into the house he might remark, with half a smile, "When the sun goes down behind a bank on Sunday night, it will rain before Wednesday night."

So you see how I came by my interest in weather, and this interest stayed with me when I left the farm in 1965 for pilot training at Webb Air Force Base near Big Spring out in West Texas. The weather at Webb was different from back home, sorta "Big Sky Country" weather, but not all that unpredictable to a Texas farm boy. Anyway, a week or two after I arrived at Webb, I was listening to the base meteorologist explain how the afternoon's flying weather was going to be "clear and fifteen" (meaning clear skies and a visibility of at least fifteen miles). It occurred to me, however, his weather forecast did not exactly match what I saw when I drove up to the Flight Shack just a few minutes before. I mentioned to Jim Cross (a good ole boy from Cumby, Texas) and some of my other pilot training buddies I thought it was going to rain that afternoon, and boy, did it ever!

This happened several more times during the summer, and my reputation as a weather predictor, who could sometimes beat the meteorologists, slowly changed to a weather conjurer who could produce rain or dust storms upon demand. My conjuring act consisted of slowly rubbing my hands together, snapping my fingers, and then pointing all ten fingers ray-like toward a promising-looking cloud.

Severe weather brought about the only respite in our grueling flying schedule, and the guys were frequently trying to get me to conjure up some weather. Since I could really only predict, rather than produce, weather, I had to be careful about my timing, but I did pretty well.

Pilot training zipped by as we learned aerobatics, navigation, formation, and instruments, and before we knew it, it was nearly Christmas. This was good news because everyone was going to get a two-week leave, our first official break since we started pilot training way back in April. We were all at a Christmas party on Thursday evening before the final scheduled day of flying on Friday when the word came down from our instructors we would only be flying the first period on Friday morning. Our instructors went on to say that in the unlikely event of inclement weather at daybreak, flying would be cancelled, and we could all go on leave a whole day early.

John Cantwell, "Tiger" Tiley, Bill Stocker, and some of the other guys immediately cornered me, and Cantwell said in a menacing voice, "OK, George let's see how good you are!" Well, this looked hopeless. I was in trouble again! The weather had been fair for several weeks, and it was very unlikely any change would occur by morning. However, they had me cornered so I decided to throw caution to the wind, so to speak. I went through my best conjuring routine, and then declared with more confidence than I felt, "It will be zero-zero in the morning." This was a pretty bold conjure since we had not seen zero ceiling and zero visibility weather during the eight months we had been at Webb. The guys seemed satisfied though and didn't bother me the rest of the evening.

Barbara and I left the party at about 10 P.M. and were sound asleep when the telephone rang about 2 A.M. When I answered, a nasal, drunken voice on the other end of the line said, "Heh, heh, George, you did it, Boy!" I eventually woke up enough to realize it was Stocker, but I couldn't figure out what he was talking about. After a few more incoherent exchanges, I finally heard Stocker say, "Look out the window, Boy!" When I pulled back the window shade, I couldn't see the street light fifty feet from the house. Heavy fog! Zero-zero weather! I had conjured it up, and it held throughout the next morning. I was a legend for the rest of the year.

The Unbelievers

"You can't really conjure weather, can you?"
—Unbelievers, 1966 to the present

The only thing wrong with telling the weather conjuring story is people invariably want to see a demonstration, like they didn't believe it or something. Well, I may have had a couple of failures, but I recall several conjures which worked even better than I planned.

On a long, hot summer day in Iowa in the mid-'70s, two of my wildlife research assistants, Gay and Lloyd Crim, and I were doing some fieldwork near Rathbun Reservoir. Gay and Lloyd had recently finished their master's degrees, and they both had keen minds. Lloyd, however, was a doubter. He was always questioning things. During a rest break, a discussion about clouds and weather inevitably led to my weather conjuring story. Lloyd, of course, wanted to see a demonstration. After the usual conjuring routine, I announced, "At least one inch of rain within two days." It actually rained about three inches within the next two hours. I hope Lloyd was satisfied.

More than ten years later when we were working on a mourning dove research project in the Lower Rio Grande Valley of Texas, I tried to conjure up some rain for U.S. Fish and Wildlife Service (USFWS) biologists Roy Tomlinson and David Dolton. It had been a particularly long, dry summer, and a bad drought was in progress. About two hours after my conjuring, a big cloud came up, and we had an impressive dust storm but only a few drops of rain. Roy and David were still poking fun at my rain-conjuring efforts several hours later when I left the Valley to return to Austin. However, that night, Roy and David, who had stayed in the Valley, were treated to a torrential six-inch rain and three tornadoes. Roy even wrote up and sent me a fake USFWS trip report stating "Mr. George's willful and audacious use of this unproven technique during such a critical period of this field study is to be condemned." From the tone of the report, I thought he was serious!

The Bible says something about "A prophet is without honor in his own country." Well, I found that must hold true for weather prophets as well. My sons, Robert and Jim, and I were sitting out in the backyard at our home in Austin, when Robert, who had heard the weather-conjuring story for years, suddenly demanded a demonstration. Well, I was in trouble again! There was only one pathetic little cumulus cloud down to the southeast, but it looked like my only hope so I did my conjure job on it. Just as I finished, there was a loud crack of thunder from the cloud! Robert glanced over at me, and said, "Hmm, message received and understood."

Finally, as I was writing an early draft of this chapter, Barbara noticed what I was doing and mentioned we had not had any appreciable rain in over two months. She then sweetly suggested this would be a good time for me to show her some weather conjuring. I did my best, and sure enough, within four hours, I managed to conjure up some dark clouds, thunder, and light rain. It was, however, the next day before a dying typhoon rolled in unexpectedly out of Mexico and drenched Central Texas.

The Campsite

"This looks like a good place to camp."
—My brother Larry, 1971

I had left the Air Force and was attending graduate school at Texas Tech University when my brother Larry, who was still in the Air Force, drove up from San Antonio, picked me up in Lubbock, and we started off for a trout fishing trip in the mountains of northern New Mexico. We had gotten a late start, and darkness overtook us by the time we had reached the foothills of the Sangre de Christi Mountains. We were both tired of driving so Larry pulled off to the side of the highway into a little plum thicket by a clump of cottonwood trees. We dug our sleeping bags out of Larry's Volvo station wagon and were soon fast asleep. A couple of hours later, I heard a distant train whistle. That sound triggered pleasant memories of trains in Commerce long ago so I rolled over and went back to sleep. A little later, the whistle sounded again, but this time it was much closer. Again, I didn't think much about it until I looked up and could see the rotating headlamp of the train rushing toward us through the trees. The train was blowing his crossing horn, and the ground was trembling. Larry and I jumped out of our sleeping bags, and began to frantically check for railroad tracks under our sleeping bags and under the vehicle. By now, the roar of the diesel engines was overwhelming, the ground was shaking, and the train's headlamp was towering above us, but we didn't know which way to run! Just as it seemed we would be struck by the train, it swooshed by us no more than eight feet away! We had just about made camp on the railroad tracks but had not realized the danger due to the thin screen of plum trees.

Later that same night, I was again awakened, but this time it sounded like a bear had invaded our campsite. I could hear a terrible growling and snuffling noise as the bear got closer and closer. I quietly unzipped my sleeping bag, reached out, and got ahold of my axe. I was about to defend myself when I realized the noise was just snoring coming from Larry's sleeping bag!

Still later that same night, Larry and I were both awakened by loud, drunken voices coming from the direction of the highway. As we sat up and looked out through our screen of plum trees, we could see a big crowd of people, on foot, pushing a car down the highway. They seemed to be having a good time. As we watched, they pushed their car up and over a low mountain pass and disappeared into the night. During the rest of the trip, Larry and I tried to find quieter campsites.

The Mongoose

"I'll tap on the box,
and maybe he'll come out."
—Jack Coffey, Wildlife Biologist, 1979

I walked into Jack Coffey's office in Chariton, Iowa, one day, and there was a small, sturdily-built animal cage sitting on the floor. There was a shipping label on the top of the cage, and neatly stenciled along one side in large letters were the words, "Danger, Live Mongoose."

As I walked over to take a closer look, I could see that the cage had two compartments. Half of the cage was solid wood, and the other half was solid wood except for a heavy, woven-wire top. As I looked down through the wire, I could see straw on the bottom of the cage and a small water dish. Toward the bottom of the solid compartment was a small hole that allowed the animal to come out into the open part of the cage.

I asked Jack what he was doing with a mongoose. He got up from his desk and came around where I was standing. He said someone had shipped it to him because he was a wildlife biologist, but he didn't know what he was going to do with it.

I wanted to see the mongoose, but Jack said it was nocturnal, very wary, and seldom came out during the day. As we were bending over the cage, Jack reached over and said, "I'll tap on the box, and maybe he'll come out." All of a sudden, there was a loud "WHACK," the top of the cage flew open, and a furry animal jumped out in my face! After I regained my composure, I realized I had been had by an adult-sized "Jack in the Box."

The top of the enclosed half of the cage was really a spring-loaded door. When Jack released the latch, the door flew open, made a loud noise, and jerked a piece of fuzzy fox tail on a string up into the air. It was pretty impressive!

Jack said he got the mongoose cage from a friend of his who was a dentist. The dentist kept it in his office, but he said he had to get rid of it. Most of his patients thought the mongoose cage was a great joke, but it nearly gave an elderly patient a heart attack. The man had trouble getting his breath, and the dentist was really concerned about him. The dentist said there was another man who seemed to be really interested in seeing the mongoose. The man said he had read that mongooses were blood-thirsty animals and that, "They go for the throat." When the dentist finally sprung the trap, the man jumped back, threw his hands up to protect his throat, and ran around the room screaming, "They go for the throat! They go for the throat!" After the dentist calmed the man down and told him it was a prank, the man wanted to whip the dentist.

Jack said if you ever want to get into trouble, get yourself a mongoose cage. He even offered me his.

Predicting Trouble

"I know something is wrong up ahead."
—Me to myself, 1972

I had never thought I had psychic powers, but beginning when I was in graduate school at Texas Tech, I found that I could sometimes accurately predict when there was trouble on the road ahead.

The first time I noticed this phenomenon, I had taken Barb and the boys for a visit with her folks in Lancaster, and I was fix'n to head back to Lubbock by myself. I got my gear packed in the car without any trouble, but when I started to leave, I had a terrible premonition that there was some sort of danger awaiting me somewhere down the road. This feeling was so strong that I didn't want to get into the car. I didn't say anything to anyone but I began delaying my planned departure. I rechecked the gear that I had packed in the trunk, checked the engine oil, and checked the air in the tires. Everyone had already said goodbye and were standing around in the driveway waiting for me to leave. After fiddling around for about five minutes, I couldn't think of anything else I could do to delay my departure without worrying everyone so I got in the car and left.

The feeling of impending danger didn't go away; it got

worse! I left Lancaster, headed north into Dallas, and west through Fort Worth. But with every turn I made and every mile I drove, the premonition of danger grew. By the time I had passed through Weatherford, I knew something was really wrong! Several miles west of Weatherford, as I approached the old steel-tresseled bridge over the Brazos River, I rounded a curve and suddenly saw the tail lights of a short line of cars stopped on the highway ahead of me. There was obviously a traffic accident up ahead. A highway patrolman had apparently just arrived on the scene, and he was directing traffic across the narrow bridge. As I passed a white sedan that was stalled on the bridge, I could see bright red blood dripping down the outside of the driver's door. Once I crossed the bridge, the feeling of danger immediately left me. If I hadn't delayed my departure by five minutes back in Lancaster, I would likely have been on the bridge at the time of the accident.

The next time I had a premonition of danger on the road, I had been working up in Northeast Iowa along the Mississippi River. I was headed back home to Boone near the middle of the state. Nearly all the roads in Iowa's farm country follow the section lines, east-west, north-south. You can't travel directly northeast to southwest on any highway, but you do have a choice of multiple hard-surfaced, farm to market roads every few miles as you zigzag across the state. I hadn't been on the road for long when I began to get the same feeling of danger that I had felt about the Brazos River accident. As I drove along, the feeling got stronger and stronger. Several times I changed my planned route and took a different road hoping to escape the feeling of doom. The feeling finally got so overwhelming, I stopped at a convenience store, got a coke, and waited about fifteen minutes. When I got back on the road, the feeling was still with me.

After a few more miles, I could see smoke in the distance. As I topped a hill, I saw where a huge gasoline tank had somehow broken loose from a semi-truck and rolled like a giant rolling pen down the highway covering the entire right-of-way from fence to fence. Several acres of roadside grass had burned off, and the tanker trailer was a charred wreck. That would not have been a good place to have been fifteen minutes earlier!

Over the years, I have had several more of these experiences, some fairly mild, some pretty impressive. The most recent experience I had like this was at night in the Texas Hill Country. I wasn't driving, but I suddenly had an extremely strong feeling of danger over the next hill. As we topped the hill, there were brake lights ahead of us and a cloud of dust. The car ahead of us had just hit a deer. Hitting a deer at night in the Texas Hill Country, the "Deer Capital of the World" is not that unusual, but not everyone can predict it just over the next hill.

Woman Trouble

"How do you handle a woman?"
"Listen well" said the wise old man.
"The way to handle a woman is to
love her, love her, simply love her."
—Wizard Merlin's advice to
young Prince Arthur
in the musical, *Camelot*

I don't know any more about women than any other
man who was raised in a family of three brothers so this
will be a short chapter. Mostly, this will be about how men
relate to women rather than the other way around.

I still don't know, for example, why the cute little girl I
hardly knew in my sixth grade Sunday School class slapped
me across the face so hard it made my ears ring. I would
have liked to have slapped her back, but my folks taught me
to never hit a woman.

That unpleasant experience at a tender age could have
marred me for life I suppose, but I didn't let it scare me too
much. My main problem in relating to females was knowing what to say. All I knew to talk about was pets and possum hunting stories. I guess some of the girls were not very
impressed because I had several one-time-only dates.

However, I eventually dated several high school and college girls, and some even let me kiss 'em.

Then a tall, slim, shapely blonde with blue-green eyes and a shy smile walked into my sophomore organic chemistry class at East Texas State College, and my life was changed forever. I quickly learned she was Miss Barbara Hejl. She was a freshman who had skipped freshman chemistry because of her high test scores. By chance, Miss Hejl was assigned as my lab partner in organic chemistry, and we got to know each other pretty well. I thought she might be somewhat aloof because of her high test scores, but she played like she needed my help in setting up her lab equipment. I asked Barbara to go out with me three times before she accepted. After our first date, I never dated another woman. She was the one!

While I was in college, my cousin Carol Fleming left her horse at the farm for a few months, and we had two horses to ride the first time I brought Barbara down to the farm. I wanted to take Barbara horseback riding so we caught both horses, put a saddle on Carol's horse, and mounted up. I was riding Lindy bareback, and I put Barbara on Carol's horse because I thought she could ride better with a saddle. We were doing all right for a while until we came across some posts lying on the ground in some weeds. Barbara's mount stopped suddenly and then jumped over the posts. This sudden stop and start unseated Barbara, and she fell off on the left side of the horse while she was still holding to the saddle horn. I glanced down and was horrified to see a large patch of prickly pear cactus directly under Barbara. Fortunately, the horse took a few more steps and cleared the cactus patch before Barbara turned loose and fell to the ground. I couldn't interest Barbara in any more horseback riding that day, but we had an adventure we still talk about. I think Barbara eventually forgave me for that first horseback ride.

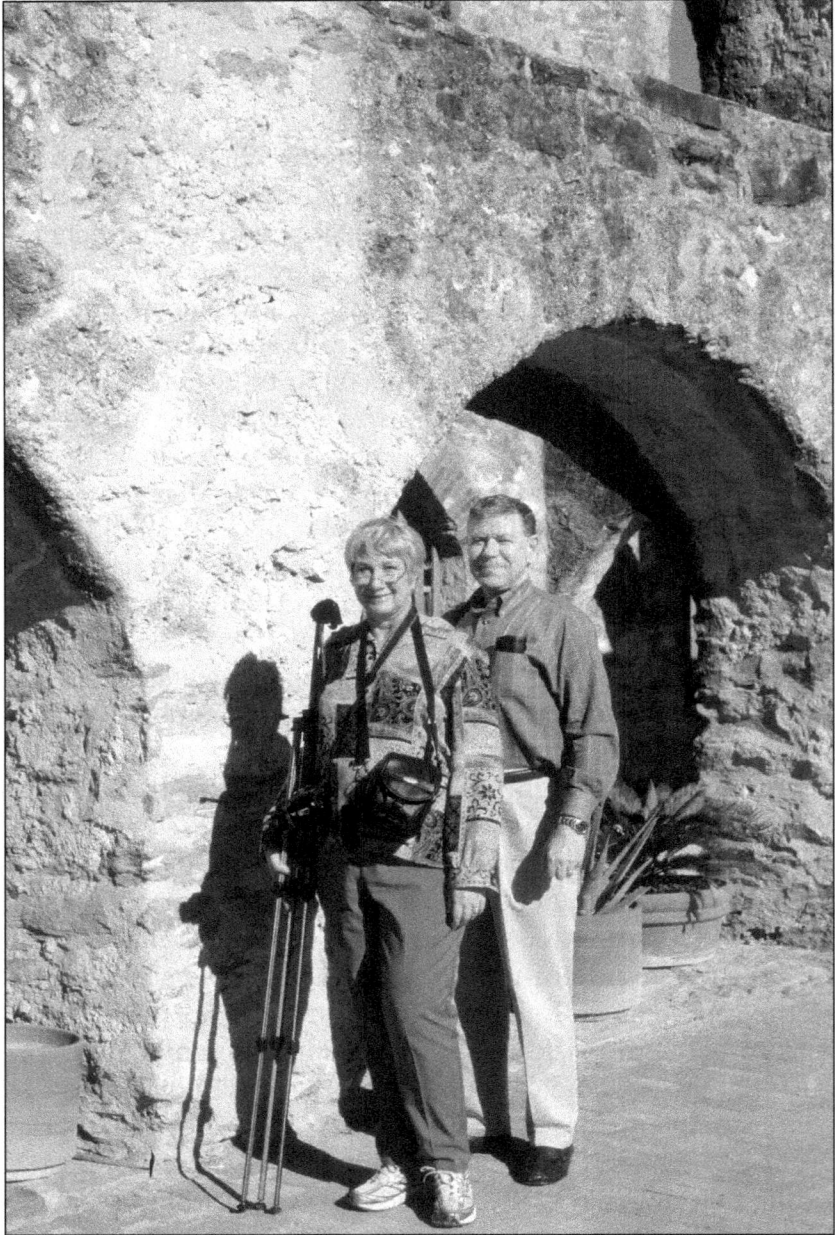

Barbara and Ron George on photography trip at Mission San Jose in San Antonio, Texas, 2006.   —Photographer unknown

Barbara and I dated for the next two years, and we were married on February 5, 1965, just after I graduated from college. Barbara left college so she could accompany me to Air Force pilot training, and she has been my wife, companion, and best friend ever since.

Air Force flying and wildlife biology were almost exclusively male occupations in my early years in those professions, and we didn't see many women in the work place. I recall when the Air Force Wing at Dyess got its first female administrative officer (an attractive brunette), and none of the guys, officers or enlisted, knew how to relate to her. Eventually, we learned she was competent and ultimately learned to treat her like any other Air Force officer, but it was a struggle at first. I understand there are now female pilots in the Air Force, and I suspect they do well, but I never met any when I was flying jets in the old days.

Later, when I was a wildlife biologist, I hired the first female conservation workers at the Wildlife Exhibit at Boone, Iowa, and some of the first female wildlife biologists who had ever worked for the Iowa Conservation Commission. I found women brought a remarkable change to this formerly all-male occupation. They worked hard, didn't complain, and did anything the guys could do.

No man is likely to be entirely immune to the charms of determined females, and I recall a time when I thought a young woman was trying to get my attention. I was coming home from work on Ben White Boulevard in Austin during rush-hour traffic. I was driving my daddy's old white 1967 Chevy pickup which we had just had repainted, and it looked pretty sharp. I was the first vehicle stopped at a red light when I noticed through my rearview mirror a woman had pulled up close behind me in her car. The setting sun, shining directly through her windshield, revealed a very attractive young woman with creamy-white complexion, long dark hair, and green eyes—a real Irish beauty, the kind

Texas deer biologist Horace Gore would call "movie star pretty." I was taking all this in, thinking rush-hour traffic wasn't so bad after all when the young woman lightly tooted her horn! Embarrassed, I looked up with a start; I assumed the light had changed, and I had missed it. But no, the light was still red. A little bit later, she tooted her horn again. Well, I didn't know what to do so I kinda waved at her while I was still looking at her through my rearview mirror. All of a sudden, she honked at me again, and I finally realized she wasn't flirting. My pickup truck was slowly rolling back on her. I was in trouble again!

One Christmas, Larry and his wife Janice and Larry's friend Bill Hammon were driving from Texas back to Pullman, Washington, where he and Bill were going to grad school at Washington State University. It was just over two thousand miles, and they were driving straight through to save on time and motel bills. Janice had a bad cold and spent the trip curled up on the back seat under a blanket. Spook, their Siamese cat, was perched on top for company. Larry and Bill hadn't heard a word from Janice for twenty-four hours or so when they stopped for gas in Tremonton, Utah, north of Salt Lake City.

Larry and Bill filled up, went to the rest room, got back in the car, glanced at the back seat where the cat was still perched on the blanket and took off. As they got to the other side of town they begin discussing where they might stop for supper. Larry turned around to ask Janice where she would like to stop. "Janice?" . . . and she wasn't there! Larry and Bill looked at each other, wheeled the car around and started back. About half way across the small town of Tremonton, a car approached and flagged them down. Janice had hitched a ride in the car and was frantically trying to catch up with them. She had gotten out of the car at the gas station to brush her teeth. All she had with her was the toothbrush; she didn't even have a coat. Neither Larry nor Bill had seen her get out. Talk about mad! She wouldn't speak to either Larry or Bill for more than two hundred miles until they finally stopped for supper in Boise. Larry surely wasn't looking for woman trouble, but he found it!

When Mike's son Zach was about to be born, Mike agreed to be with his wife Sharon during the delivery. Everything was going fine at first, but the delivery became complicated. A nurse noticed Mike was getting paler by the minute. She lead Mike out in the hall where he had to lean against the wall. The next thing Mike knew, he had slid down the wall and passed out on the floor. Sharon said, "Men don't know nothing about birthing no babies."

Office Trouble

"My word, Ron!"
—Bob Cook,
Wildlife Division Director

You would think that I would eventually grow up and learn to stay out of trouble, but one day a map tube arrived in the mail. I was in my office at Texas Parks and Wildlife Department Headquarters in Austin when someone sent me several maps all rolled up in a thirty-inch long, four-inch diameter cardboard mailing tube. No one can get in trouble with a mailing tube can they? I can assure you one of the George boys can.

As I pulled the two halves of the mailing tube apart to remove the maps, I noticed there was a tremendous amount of suction holding the two halves together. Once I got the maps out, I saw that there was another long cardboard tube that fit snuggly inside the full length of the two halves. This super tight fit was what was causing the suction as I pulled the tubes apart. I didn't think much about it until I tried to put the tubes back together. There was just as much resistance in closing the tubes as there had been in opening them. In fact, as I pushed the two tubes together, my hands slipped, and the tubes jumped apart a little ways. Well, that was interesting. It was a slow morning so I wondered what

Wildlife biologist Ron George using airboat to collect ducks for a waterfowl lead-poisoning study, 1984.　　　　　　—Photo by Charles Stutzenbaker

would happen if I put one end of the tube on the floor and really pushed down on the top end.

When I executed this scientific experiment, there as a very loud "POW!" One of the admin techs just over the partition wall screamed, "EEK!" and nothing else happened. No one came to see what the noise was about, said "Are you all right?" or anything.

I looked around my office and found the bottom half and the long inside sleeve of the mailing tube, but I couldn't see the top half anywhere. Finally, I looked up at the suspended foamboard ceiling and saw a perfectly round, four-inch diameter hole in the ceiling. Well, I was kinda embarrassed. Here I was supposed to be a supervisor and setting a good example for the employees, but I had left some clear evidence of the mischief of my idle hands. I assumed the first person who walked into my office would see the hole in the ceiling. After all, the black hole in the white ceiling looked big enough for a stove pipe. Surprisingly, no one even noticed it. After several days, I told my boss Bob Cook what I had done and showed him the hole in the ceiling. Bob looked up and said, "My word, Ron!"

Bob had the maintenance folks bring me a new ceiling tile and retrieve the other half of my mailing tube. That should have been the end of the story, but here we are dealing with one of the George boys.

I took the mailing tube home and repeated the experiment in my backyard. I got out in the open away from any trees, placed the bottom end of the tube on a stone sidewalk, and got the mailing tube sections all in place. I moved my head well out of the way and pushed down really hard on the top of the mailing tube. Again, there was a loud "POW!" When, I looked up to see how high the tube had gone, I had trouble seeing it. If you have ever shot an arrow straight up in the air and watched it disappear, you will have some idea of what that mailing tube looked like.

Still Looking for Trouble

"You won't belive this, but an aircraft
has just flown into the World Trade Center!"
—Air Traffic Controller, 9/11/2001

After my Air Force years, I earned a masters degree in Range and Wildlife Science at Texas Tech University in 1972 and spent the next thirty-three years as a wildlife biologist in Iowa and Texas. I learned to spotlight pheasants, rope rattlesnakes, drive mice, radio-collar mountain lions, and burn houses. I've met three Texas governors and worked with a lot of great people. I heard the space shuttle *Columbia* blow up over Northeast Texas on February 1, 2003, and had a small part in coordinating some of the recovery efforts. I am now retired and enjoy reading, gardening, photography, hunting, fishing, travel, and visiting with friends. My wife Barbara and I live in Austin, Texas.

After Larry retired from the Air Force, he continued to work in the biomedical field under contract with the military at Biloxi, Mississippi. When I heard that Hurricane Katrina was threatening the Biloxi area in August 2005, I called Larry on his cell phone at 8 A.M. the morning the hurricane was coming ashore to see if he and his family were all right. He said they were just about ready to evacuate their home because the water was already up in their yard. I knew his yard was about fourteen feet above sea level, so that sounded pretty scary to me. Larry said he had to go and abruptly hung up. Although I tried to get in touch with him repeatedly over the next several days, we didn't hear anything more from them until communications were restored more than a week later.

Larry said they had traveled east from Biloxi on Interstate 10 to the Alabama stateline and avoided the worst of the hurricane, but they eventually had two flat tires from roofing-shingle nails and a car window knocked out by flying debris (a fairly unusual road trip even for one of the George boys). When Larry and his family finally got back home, they found there had been five feet of sea water in the bottom floor of their two-story house. Their grand piano, grandfather clocks, computers, kitchen cabinets, sheetrock walls, and everything else in the downstairs was ruined. I went down to help them twice, but it took them over two years to restore their flooded home.

After Mike left the Air Force, he got a job as an airline pilot with Piedmont Airlines, which later merged with U.S. Air. Over the years, he flew YS-11s "Rice Rockets," Boeing 727s and 737s, and later Airbuses. At 8 A.M. on the morning of September 11, 2001, U.S. Airways Captain Mike George took off from Charlotte, North Carolina, at the controls of an Airbus 321 bound for Seattle. He had a full load of passengers and fuel. They had only been airborne a hour or so when Air Traffic Control (ATC) said in the clear over the radio, "You won't believe this, but an aircraft has just flown into the World Trade Center!" Mike's first officer quickly checked the weather at New York's LaGuardia Airport, noted the completely clear weather, turned to Mike and said, "Well, it wasn't an accident." A little bit later, ATC said, "You won't believe this, but a second aircraft has flown into the World Trade Center!" Mike's aircraft was

Piedmont Airlines Captain Mike George with Boeing 727, Greensboro, North Carolina, 1985. —Photo by author

then informed that a national emergency had been declared, and they were ordered to land at St. Louis. Mike still flies today for U.S. Airways. He and his wife Sharon live in Brunswick, Georgia.

Our parents have passed away, but Larry, Mike, and I still own the Farm on Timber Creek. We try to get up there several times a year, meet some old friends, and see what kind of trouble we can get into. We don't climb as high in the trees as we once did, and we don't swim with the snakes anymore. We haven't boated down Timber Creek in a horse trough in a long time, and we haven't swiped a watermelon in years.

We can, however, still chainsaw some firewood, repair fences, spray brush, and get a tractor stuck in the mud. We can also find poison ivy, trip over barbed wire, step in armadillo holes, and occasionally let a fire get away from us.

We still enjoy fishing and shooting our guns. Mostly though, we just like to walk around on the place, talk about the old days, and marvel that we have been so fortunate. They say the Good Lord looks out for fools, drunks, and little kids. I guess we still qualify.

George boys on javelina hunt in South Texas with Daddy's 1967 Chevy pickup, 1996. —Photo by Jim George

In trouble again! Larry and Mike digging tractor out of mud at the farm, 2003.
—Photo by author

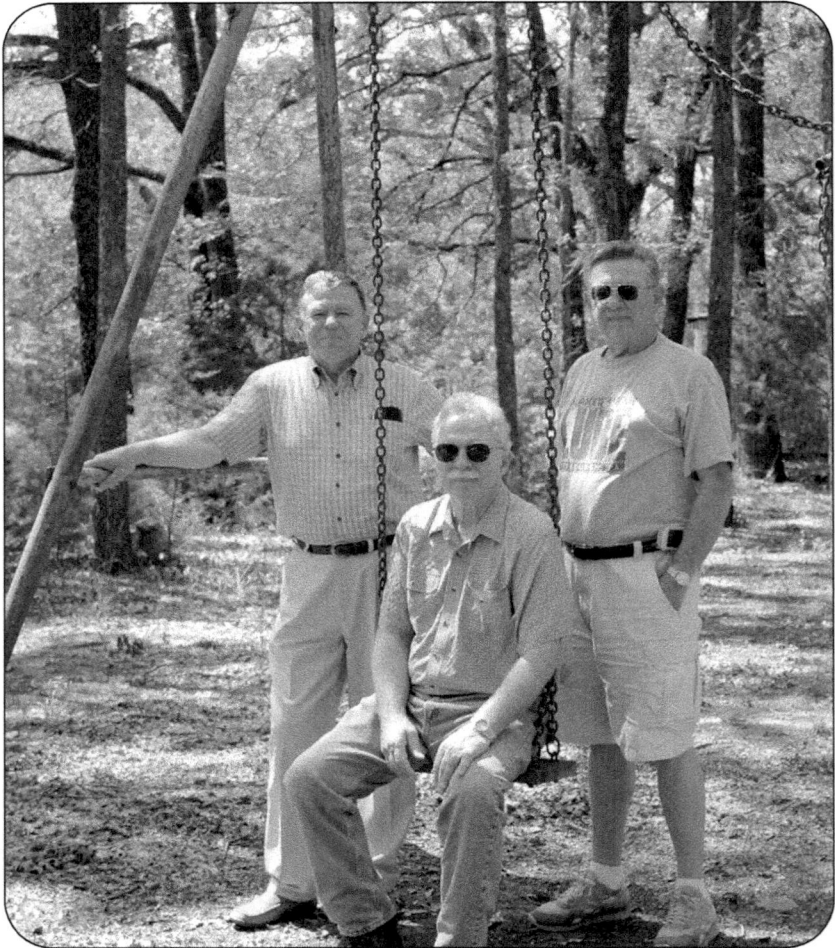

Still looking for trouble—Ron, Mike, and Larry with their old swing set at the Farm on Timber Creek, 2007. —Photo by Barbara George

About the Author

RON GEORGE grew up around the small towns, farms, railroad yards, and airfields of Northeast Texas. He graduated from Greenville High School in 1961 and received a B.S. degree in general science at East Texas State University in Commerce in 1965.

Ron is a former U.S. Air Force captain, jet tanker pilot, and Vietnam veteran. He served in Alaska, Greenland, Newfoundland, Okinawa, and Southeast Asia. During 1968, Ron and his crew flew twenty-eight combat missions

Ron George
—Photo by
Barbara George

and logged more than two hundred hours of combat airtime in their unarmed KC-135 jet tanker aircraft refueling American fighters and bombers striking targets in North Vietnam. They witnessed the communist "Tet Offensive" in South Vietnam and participated in the *"Pueblo* Incident" in Korea. His military decorations include the Air Medal, the Vietnam Service Medal, and the Armed Forces Expedi-

tionary Medal. Ron's book about his Air Force adventures is entitled *Airspeed, Altitude, and a Sense of Humor*.

Ron left the Air Force in 1970 and completed a master's degree in range and wildlife management at Texas Tech University. He served as a wildlife biologist in Iowa and later in Texas for more than thirty-three years. He is a Past-President of the Texas Chapter of The Wildlife Society and Past-Chairman of the Migratory Shore and Upland Game Bird Subcommittee of the International Association of Fish and Wildlife Agencies. Ron has been an invited guest lecturer on wildlife conservation in the People's Republic of China. He is the author or co-author of more than sixty publications on wildlife science. His popular book about his unique adventures as a wildlife biologist is entitled *Of Mice and Mountain Lions*.

Ron was selected as the Outstanding Alumnus of the Department of Range and Wildlife Management at Texas Tech University in 1988 and a Distinguished Alumnus of the College of Agricultural Sciences and Natural Resources at Texas Tech University in 2000.

Ron retired in 2005 as the Deputy Director of the Wildlife Division, Texas Parks and Wildlife Department. He and his wife Barbara live in Austin, Texas.